Samsung®
Galaxy Tabs

for
dummies®
A Wiley Brand

Samsung® Galaxy Tabs

by Dan Gookin

A Wiley Brand

Samsung® Galaxy Tabs For Dummies®

Published by: **John Wiley & Sons, Inc.**, 111 River Street, Hoboken, NJ 07030-5774, www.wiley.com

For general information on our other products and services, please contact our Customer Care Department within the U.S. at 877-762-2974, outside the U.S. at 317-572-3993, or fax 317-572-4002. For technical support, please visit https://hub.wiley.com/community/support/dummies.

Wiley publishes in a variety of print and electronic formats and by print-on-demand. Some material included with standard print versions of this book may not be included in e-books or in print-on-demand. If this book refers to media such as a CD or DVD that is not included in the version you purchased, you may download this material at http://booksupport.wiley.com. For more information about Wiley products, visit www.wiley.com.

Library of Congress Control Number: 2018965298

ISBN 978-1-119-46660-4 (pbk); ISBN 978-1-119-46659-8 (ebk); ISBN 978-1-119-46658-1 (ebk)

Manufactured in the United States of America

V10007191_122718

Contents at a Glance

Table of Contents

Introduction

The Samsung Galaxy Tab is an excellent choice for enhancing your 21st century, mobile digital life. The tablet is a remarkable gizmo, one that's capable of doing so much. Samsung packed a lot of potential into the device. One thing they didn't pack were any instructions. Yes, despite its impressive power, the Galaxy Tab can be a confusing, intimidating piece of hardware.

Relax.

You hold in your hand a great resource, companion, and guide to your Galaxy Tab. The purpose here is to help you get the most from your tablet, without scaring the bejeebers out of you.

About This Book

Still reading? Great! So few people bother with the introduction in any book that I'm amazed you bothered to keep going. Honestly, I could write how to turn lead into gold in this paragraph and you'd be one of six people on the planet to ever read it. Count yourself fortunate. And handsome. I mean, why not?

This book is a reference. It's written to help you get the most from your Galactic tablet. Each chapter covers a specific topic, and the sections in each chapter address an issue related to the topic. The overall idea is to show how to do things on the tablet and to help you get the most from it without overwhelming you with information or intimidating you into despair.

Sample sections in this book include

>> Making a home for the tablet

>> Touring the Home screen

>> Typing quickly by using predictive text

>> Placing a Skype phone call

>> Running Facebook on your tablet

» Recording video

» Turning lead into gold

» Find your lost tablet

Did you notice that one of those items is fake? That's because you're still reading the Introduction and I'm proud of you for sticking with it.

This book explains all topics carefully. Everything is cross-referenced. Technical terms and topics, when they come up, are neatly shoved to the side, where they're easily avoided. The idea here isn't to learn anything. This book's philosophy is to help you look it up, figure it out, and get on with your life.

This book follows a few conventions for using a Galaxy Tab. First of all, I refer to your device as the Galaxy Tab or just Tab throughout the book. I might also write *Galaxy tablet* or even, occasionally, *Galactic tablet*. Generally speaking, all the information here applies to the Galaxy Tab S4.

The way you interact with the tablet is by using its *touchscreen*. The device also has some physical buttons, found below the touchscreen. It also features some holes and connectors. All those items are described in Chapter 1. You can touch the screen in various ways, which are explained and named in Chapter 3.

Chapter 4 discusses tablet text input, which involves using an onscreen keyboard. You can also input text by speaking to the tablet, which is also covered in Chapter 4.

This book directs you to do things by following numbered steps. Each step involves a specific activity, such as touching something on the screen; for example:

1. **Choose Downloads.**

This step directs you to touch the text or item labeled *Downloads* on the screen. You might also be told to do this:

2. **Tap Downloads.**

 Some On–Off features are activated by using the Master Control icon, similar to what's shown in the margin. When the circle is to the right, the feature is on. You can either tap the icon or slide it a wee bit by dragging your finger on the touchscreen.

Foolish Assumptions

Even though this book is written with the gentle handholding required by anyone who is just starting out or who is easily intimidated, I've made a few assumptions. For example, I assume that you're a human being and not the emperor of Jupiter. See? You're getting all this comedy gold just from sticking to reading the introduction. (I'm gonna write my mom about this.)

My biggest assumption: You have a Samsung Galaxy tablet, such as the Tab S4. Other Tab model users can get good information from this book, though it doesn't specifically cover those tablet versions.

A Tab that accesses the mobile data (cellular) network is called an LTE Tab, where LTE stands for Long Term Evolution or something. It doesn't matter. The other Tab is known as a Wi-Fi–only tab. Any differences between the two types of Tabs are pointed out in the text.

You don't need a computer to use this book, although having one does let you do certain things. The computer can be a desktop or a laptop, and a PC or a Macintosh. Oh, I suppose it could also be a Linux computer. In any event, I refer to the computer as "a computer" throughout this book. When directions are specific to a PC or a Mac, the book says so.

Finally, this book doesn't assume that you have a Google account, but having one helps. Information is provided in Chapter 2 about setting up a Google account — an extremely important part of using the Galaxy Tab. Having a Google account opens up a slew of useful features, information, and programs that make using your tablet more productive.

Icons Used in This Book

TIP

This icon flags useful, helpful tips or shortcuts.

REMEMBER

This icon marks a friendly reminder to do something.

WARNING

This icon marks a friendly reminder not to do something.

TECHNICAL STUFF

This icon alerts you to overly nerdy information and technical discussions of the topic at hand. Reading the information is optional, though it may win you the Daily Double on *Jeopardy!*

Beyond the Book

Bonus information for this title can be found online. You can visit the publisher's website to find an online Cheat Sheet. Go to www.dummies.com and type Samsung Galaxy Tabs For Dummies Cheat Sheet into the Search box. Cross your fingers and click the Search button on the web page. The online Cheat Sheet should appear in mere Internet moments.

I also do my own helpful updates, blog posts, and alerts, which are also free but far more engaging. My stuff is updated more frequently than the publisher's website because (last time I checked) I'm not a big corporation. You can find my own information at

www.wambooli.com

My email address is dgookin@wambooli.com. Yes, that's my real address. I reply to all email I get, and you'll get a quick reply if you keep your question short and specific to this book. Although I do enjoy saying "Hi," I cannot answer technical support questions, resolve billing issues, or help you troubleshoot your Galaxy Tab. Thanks for understanding.

Enjoy this book and your Galactic tablet!

Where to Go from Here

Hey! Thanks for hanging in there. Now I fully expect you to read the entire book, cover to cover, including the loopy ads at the end. *Chihuahuas For Dummies*? Are they serious?

Back to the topic at hand: Start reading! Observe the table of contents and find something that interests you. Or look up your puzzle in the index. When these suggestions don't cut it, just start reading Chapter 1.

1

A Galaxy at Your Fingertips

Chapter **1**

Tab Orientation

I thoroughly enjoy getting a new gizmo and opening its box. Expectations build. Joy is released. Then despair descends, like a grand piano pushed out of a third-story window. That's because using any new electronic device, especially something as sophisticated as the Samsung Galaxy Tab, can be frustrating and confusing. You have a lot of ground to cover. To make your journey easier, I offer this gentle introduction.

Set Up Your Galaxy Tab

Most Galaxy tablets patiently wait in their box for your attention. The exception is the cellular, or LTE, tablet. Because it uses the mobile data signal, the kind people at the Phone Store might have worked through a setup-and-configuration process with you. This step is necessary to get the mobile data network up and running. For non-cellular, or Wi-Fi-only, tablets, the initial configuration and you are awkward strangers on a blind date.

» Chapter 2 specifically covers the setup process as well as basic on-off procedures.

» An LTE tablet is one that uses the mobile data network to access the Internet, the same as a smartphone. Yes, you pay monthly for that service.

>> A Wi-Fi–only tablet uses only a Wi-Fi network for Internet access. LTE tablets can also use Wi-Fi for Internet access. See Chapter 17 for information on configuring your tablet for use with a Wi-Fi network.

>> The initial setup of an LTE tablet identifies the device with the mobile data network, giving it a network ID and associating the ID with your cellular bill.

Opening the box

Liberate your Galaxy Tab from its box by locating and lifting the cardboard tab. Gleefully remove any plastic sheeting that clings to the device. Check the sides, edges, front, and back. Also check the rear camera lens to ensure that it's not covered with plastic.

In the box's bottom compartment, you may find:

>> **A USB cable:** You can use it to connect the tablet to a computer or a wall charger.

>> **A wall charger:** You'll find a USB connector (hole) on the charger as well as metal prongs for plugging the thing into a wall socket.

>> **The S-Pen:** This digital stylus allows for precise touchscreen input. You can use it instead of your stubby finger to draw images, write text, or manipulate graphical goobers.

>> **Pamphlets with warnings and warranty information:** I find it amazing that the *Getting Started* pamphlet is about 2 percent of the size of the warnings and warranty information. I blame the discrepancy on lawyers, who are obviously better than technology writers at getting work.

>> **The 4G SIM card holder:** For the LTE/cellular tablet, you need a 4G SIM card. The Phone Store employee may have tossed its holder into the box as well. You can throw it out.

>> **Delicious air:** Most of the inside of the box is air, bringing you the yummy odors of the Samsung manufacturing plant in Asia.

Go ahead and free the USB cable and power charger from their clear plastic cocoons. That's because the next step is to charge the tablet's battery, covered in the following section.

>> Refer to Chapter 5 for details on using the S Pen as well as the optional book cover keyboard.

>> Keep the box for as long as you own your tablet. If you ever need to return the device or ship it somewhere, the original box is the ideal container. You can shove the useless pamphlets and papers back into the box as well.

Charging the battery

The first thing that I recommend you do with your Galaxy Tab is to give it a full charge. Obey these steps:

1. **Plug one end of the USB cable into the wall adapter.**

2. **Attach the other end of the USB cable to the tablet.**

   The cable attaches to the tablet's edge — usually, the bottom edge, though it can be on the side. The USB connector (hole) cannot be mistaken, and the cable plugs in only one way.

3. **Plug the wall adapter into the wall.**

Upon success, you may see a Battery icon on the tablet's touchscreen. The icon gives you an idea of the device's current battery-power level and lets you know that the tablet is functioning properly. Don't be alarmed if the Battery icon fails to appear.

If the Welcome screen appears as you charge the tablet, you can proceed with the initial configuration, which is covered in Chapter 2. Or you can wait and finish reading this chapter first. Or have a cookie. It's always fun to ignore responsibility and have a cookie.

>> Most tablets come partially charged from the factory. That's no excuse! I recommend giving your tablet a good initial charge. It also helps you to become familiar with the process.

>> The USB cable can also be used to connect the Galaxy Tab to a computer. See Chapter 18 for details.

TIP

>> The tablet's battery charges when the tablet is plugged into a computer's USB port, though it's not as effective as charging with a wall socket.

>> The Galaxy Tab does not have a removable, and therefore replaceable, battery.

Know Your Way around the Galaxy

"Second star to the right and straight on 'till morning" may get Peter Pan to Neverland, but you need more specific directions for navigating your way around the Galaxy Tab.

Finding things on the tablet

Many interesting and useful items festoon the front, back, and perimeter of your Galaxy Tab. Before going into detail, I must address the issue of which way is up on your tablet.

As far as the touchscreen goes, the image orients itself properly no matter how you hold the tablet. For reference purposes, however, the front-facing camera identifies the top of the device, as illustrated in Figure 1-1.

Camera

Camera

Horizontal orientation

FIGURE 1-1: Galaxy Tab orientations.

Vertical orientation

For older Tabs, the physical Home button dwells on the bottom edge, along with navigation buttons stenciled onto the tablet's bezel.

Now that I've clarified which way is up, take a moment to peruse the following list and locate the items mentioned on your tablet.

Touchscreen display: The biggest part of the tablet is its touchscreen display, which occupies almost all the territory on the front of the device. The touchscreen display is a see-touch thing: You look at it and also touch it with your fingers to control the tablet. See Chapter 3 for details on touchscreen manipulation.

Front camera: The tablet's front-facing camera is centered above the touchscreen. The camera is used for taking self-portraits as well as for video chats. See Chapter 12 for information on using your Galaxy Tab as a camera; Chapter 8 covers video chat.

Light sensor: Just next to the front camera is a teensy light sensor. It helps to adjust the brightness level of the touchscreen.

TIP

Power/USB connector: The Power/USB jack is typically located on the tablet's bottom edge, though some tabs may stick it on the side. This location is where you attach the USB cable to the tablet.

Power Lock key: The Power Lock key is the smaller of two thin buttons on the edge of the device. Press Power Lock to turn on the tablet, to lock it (put it to sleep), to wake it up, and to turn it off. Directions for performing these tasks are found in Chapter 2.

Volume key: The tablet's Volume key is found next to the Power Lock key; it's the longer of the two. Press one side of the key to set the volume louder, and press the other side to set the volume lower.

Headphone jack: The tablet's largest hole accommodates a standard headphone plug. This is where you connect headphones to the tablet.

SIM card cover: This spot is used to access an LTE tablet's SIM card, and it's found only on LTE tablets.

Media card slot: Use this slot to add or remove a microSD memory card. See the next section.

IR Blaster: This port has a great name but a rather mundane function: It sends an infrared signal to another device, such as a TV, *if* the tablet has the proper app installed.

Speaker(s): Stereo speakers are located on opposite edges on the tablet, though smaller tablets put the speakers on the back.

Microphone: A tiny hole on the tablet serves as the device's microphone. The hole's location may not be apparent — it's about the diameter of a pinhead — but it's there. Avoid the temptation to stick anything into that wee li'l hole.

Rear camera and flash: The rear camera is found on the back of the tablet. If your Galaxy Tab camera features a flash, the flash LED is found nearby.

TECHNICAL STUFF

>> Be careful not to confuse the SIM card with the removable storage media (microSD) card. They're not the same thing. You'll rarely, if ever, access the SIM card.

>> SIM stands for Subscriber Identity Module. The SIM card is used by your cellular provider to identify your tablet and keep track of the amount of data it accesses. Yep, that's so you can be billed properly. The SIM also gives your cellular tablet a phone number, though that's merely an account number and not something you can dial or send a text message to.

Inserting and removing a microSD card

Expand your tablet's storage capacity by installing a microSD card. The card stores photos, music, and other information, supplementing the device's internal storage. You can also use the card to exchange files between the tablet and other devices, such as a computer.

The microSD card can be inserted whether the device is on or off. Heed these directions:

1. **Locate the microSD card hatch on the tablet's edge.**

Figure 1-2 illustrates the hatch's appearance, though it may look subtly different on your tablet.

SD Card tray

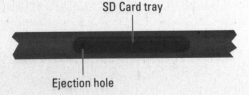

FIGURE 1-2:
The microSD
card cover.

Ejection hole

2. **Press an unbent paperclip or another "pokey" implement into the hole on the hatch cover.**

Upon success, the hatch pops up. Grab the hatch and remove the tray.

Some older tablets feature a hatch with a thumbnail slot instead of a pokey hole. This type of slot cover doesn't come off completely.

3. **Orient the microSD card and set it into the tray.**

For the older-style slots, ensure that the microSD card's printed side is up and the teeny triangle on the card is pointing toward the open slot.

4. **Insert the tray into the slot or otherwise push the card into the slot.**

If the tablet is on (and has been configured), you may see a prompt informing you that the card has been inserted.

To remove the microSD card, follow these steps:

1. **If the tablet is on, unmount the microSD card; otherwise, skip to Step 2.**

Before you attempt this process, reading Chapters 2 and 3 helps.

a. *Open the Settings app.*

b. *Choose Device Maintenance.*

c. *Tap Storage.*

d. *Tap the Action Overflow (the three vertical dots in the upper right corner of the touchscreen) and choose Storage Settings.*

e. *Tap the Eject icon next to the SD Card item.*

A message appears briefly on the touchscreen, telling you that it's okay to remove the microSD card; proceed with Step 2.

2. **Open the microSD card slot.**

Specific directions are offered earlier in this section.

3. **Remove the microSD card from its tray.**

When the tablet is turned off, you can insert or remove the microSD card at will. Refer to Chapter 2 for information on turning off your Galaxy Tab.

WARNING

» You cannot unmount the microSD card when the tablet is connected to a computer. Disconnect the tablet and try again.

» Odds are good that your tablet didn't come with a microSD card, so run out and buy one!

» The microSD cards are teensy. To use the card on a computer or another electronic device, get a microSD card adapter.

» The Galaxy Tab accepts microSD cards up to 64GB in capacity. You'll find less expensive microSD cards in capacities of 16GB and 32GB.

>> GB is an abbreviation for *gigabyte,* which is 1 billion characters of storage. One gigabyte is enough storage for about an hour of video or a week's worth of music or a year's worth of photographs. It's a lot of storage.

>> And if you're curious: SD stands for Secure Digital.

>> The tablet works with or without a microSD card installed.

>> Refer to Chapter 18 for more information on storage.

Getting optional accessories

You need not buy all your galactic gear from Samsung or the place where you purchased your Tab. Plenty of accessories are available. Of the lot, I recommend the following:

Earphones: You can use earphones from any standard smartphone or portable media player with your tablet. Plug the earphones into the tablet's headphone jack and you're ready to go.

Bluetooth keyboard: Your Galaxy Tab works with any Bluetooth keyboard. It gives you the option of using a real keyboard with the device. Even keyboards for those i-fruit company tablets work with your tablet.

Vehicle charger: Use a vehicle charger to charge the tablet while in your car. This adapter plugs into the car's 12-volt power supply, in the receptacle once known as the cigarette lighter. The vehicle charger is a must-have item if you plan to use the Galaxy tablet navigation features in your auto or you need a charge on the road.

>> None of this extra stuff is essential to using the tablet.

>> If the earphones feature a microphone, you can use the microphone for dictation and audio recording on the tablet.

>> If the earphones feature a button, you can use the button to pause and play music. Press the button once to pause and again to play.

>> See Chapter 17 for more information on pairing your tablet with a Bluetooth keyboard. Details on using the official Samsung Galaxy Tab accessories are found in Chapter 5.

Where to Keep Your Tab

Like your car keys, glasses, wallet, and time travel return anklet, you'll want to keep your Galaxy tablet in a place where it's safe, easy to find, and always handy whether you're at home, at work, on the road, or watching Caesar's triumphant return from Gaul.

Making a home for the tablet

I recommend keeping your Galaxy Tab in the same spot when you've finished using it. My first suggestion is to make a place next to your computer. Keep the charging cord handy, or just plug the cord into the computer's USB port so that you can synchronize information with your computer regularly and keep the tablet charged.

Another nifty place to keep the tablet is on your nightstand. See Chapter 15 for information on using the tablet to satisfy your nighttime reading or video watching. It can also serve as an alarm clock.

Avoid keeping the tablet anyplace where it may get too hot. Avoid setting it on a windowsill or on a car dashboard or anywhere in direct sunlight for prolonged periods.

Keep the tablet visible. Don't put it where someone might sit on it, step on it, or otherwise damage it. And don't leave the tablet under a stack of newspapers on a table or a counter, where it might get accidentally tossed out or recycled.

Never leave your tablet unattended on the planet Venus.

REMEMBER

As long as you return the tablet to the same spot when you're done with it, you'll always know where it is.

Taking the tablet with you

If you're like me, you probably carry your Galactic tablet with you around the house, in the office, at the airport, in the air, or in the car. I hope you're not using the tablet while you're driving! Regardless, have a portable place to store your tablet while you're on the road.

The ideal storage spot for the tablet is in the book cover keyboard or any other carrying case or pouch specially designed for the Galaxy Tab. A case keeps the tablet from being dinged, scratched, or even unexpectedly turned on while it's in your backpack, purse, carry-on luggage, or wherever you put the tablet when you aren't using it.

Also see Chapter 22 for information on using your Galaxy Tab on the road.

Chapter **2**

The On-and-Off Chapter

In the book *Lamps For Dummies*, the chapter for turning a lamp on or off is barely a page long. That's because lamps haven't changed much in the past 100 years; they still have two modes — on and off. You would think that turning a Galaxy Tab on and off would require similar brevity. Alas, that's not the case.

For starters, the tablet lacks an on–off switch. Instead, it offers a Power Lock key, which serves multiple functions. Next, multiple options are available for dismissing the tablet. Unlike when turning off a lamp, you can turn off, restart, or lock your Tab. These features, which are necessary for a sophisticated piece of technology, require that this chapter be more than a page long.

Hello, Tablet

Turning on the Galaxy Tab is fairly simple: Press and hold down the Power Lock button. Eventually the touchscreen comes to life, impressing you with Samsung's start-up graphics and sound. Short. Sweet. Simple.

Sadly, there's more to the story than short, sweet, and simple.

REMEMBER

The tablet won't start unless the battery is charged. See Chapter 1.

Turning on your Galaxy Tab (for the first time)

The very, very first time your Galaxy tablet is turned on is a special event. That's when you configure the device, answering various questions and setting a few basic options. After this ordeal, turning on the tablet is fast and easy; see the later section "Turning on your tablet."

The initial setup involves several steps, which may change after this book goes to press. I recommend reading the following list to familiarize yourself with the process; then use the steps as a reference if you need assistance:

1. **Press the Power Lock key to turn on the tablet.**

   You may have to press the button longer than you think; when the tablet's logo appears on the screen, release the button.

   It's okay to turn on the tablet while it's plugged in and charging.

TIP

2. **Choose a language.**

   Yes, if you're reading this in English, you choose English as the language for your tablet.

3. **Activate the cellular tablet.**

   This step was most likely done at the Phone Store. If it wasn't, follow the directions on the screen and wait for the connection to be established.

4. **Connect to a Wi-Fi network.**

   Choose an available Wi-Fi network from the list. Type the password. Tap the Connect button. More detailed steps are provided in Chapter 17.

   Even if you have a cellular Galaxy Tab, connect to a Wi-Fi network, if one is available. Using Wi-Fi incurs no fees, unlike the mobile data connection.

5. **Agree to the terms and conditions.**

   Touch the box to place or remove the check marks as prompted.

6. **Sign in to your Google account.**

   You can always associate your Google account later, but get it out of the way now. If you don't have a Google account, sign up for one. See the later section "More Accounts for Your Tab."

TIP

7. **Answer other questions as prompted.**

   Many of the settings are optional. Look for the SKIP button to perform various setup options later.

8. **Tap the Finish button when setup is complete.**

   You can now use your tablet.

The good news is that you're done. Setup is a process you endure only once on the Galaxy Tab. From this point on, starting the tablet works as described in the next few sections.

Exception: You may have to endure a cavalcade of updates after starting your tablet for the very first time. Proceed with installing any given updates. I recommend keeping the tablet plugged in. Obey the prompts on the screen.

Don't be surprised when you see multiple updates. This happens often when you first activate an Android tablet.

>> If you use other Android devices, choose the option to restore your account. This choice installs many of your favorite apps and settings. It doesn't remove your account from the other device.

>> You do not need a Samsung account to use the Galaxy Tab.

>> See the nearby sidebar "Who is this Android person?" for more information about the Android operating system.

Turning on your tablet

To turn on the Galaxy Tab, press and hold down the Power Lock button. After a few seconds, you see the tablet's start-up logo and then some hypnotic animation. The tablet is coming to life.

Eventually, you see the unlock screen. See the later section "Working the Lock screen" for details on what to do next.

Unlocking the tablet

It's natural for the Galaxy Tab to be on and locked. The device is working, but the touchscreen is off, similar to a computer put into Sleep mode. The tablet operates this way when you're not actively using it. Its battery supports keeping the device on and locked for lengthy periods.

WHO IS THIS ANDROID PERSON?

Just like a computer, your Samsung tablet has an operating system. It's the main program in charge of all the software, or apps, inside the tablet. Unlike on a computer, however, Android is a mobile device operating system, designed primarily for use in tablets and smartphones.

Android is based on the Linux operating system, which is also a computer operating system. Linux is much more stable than Windows and it's bug-free, so it's not as popular. Google owns, maintains, and develops Android, which is why your online Google information is synced with the Galaxy Tab. The Android mascot, shown here, often appears on Android apps or hardware. He has no official name, though most folks call him Andy.

Choose any of these techniques to unlock the tablet:

>> Press the Power Lock button. Unlike when turning on the tablet, a quick press is all that's needed.

>> Open the book cover keyboard, if it's installed.

>> Connect or disconnect the USB cable (when the cable is supplying power).

After unlocking the tablet, you see the Lock screen. Work the screen lock as described in the next section to start using the device.

The tablet automatically locks whenever it's bored or after you've ignored it for a while. While locked, the touchscreen turns off to save power. See the section "Locking the tablet," later in this chapter, for information on how to manually lock the tablet.

Working the Lock screen

The Galaxy Tab has several locks for its Lock screen. These locks provide extra security, though most of the locks aren't considered all that secure. Here are the available locks:

Swipe: The standard screen lock. Swipe your finger on the screen to unlock the device, as illustrated in Figure 2-1.

Lock screen notifications

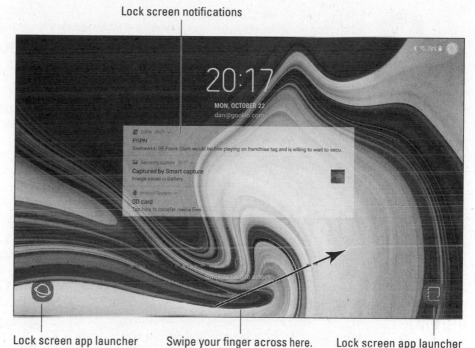

FIGURE 2-1:
The basic
unlocking screen.

Lock screen app launcher   Swipe your finger across here.   Lock screen app launcher

Pattern: Trace a preset pattern over the nine dots on the screen.

PIN: Type a number to unlock the device.

Password: Type a password, which can include letters, numbers, and symbols.

None: The device features no Lock screen; you can use the tablet immediately.

One of these locks appears whenever you turn on or unlock the tablet. Or, in the case of the None setting, no lock appears.

REMEMBER

>> The most secure lock types are PIN and Password. The Pattern lock is moderately secure, though not foolproof. The None and Swipe settings are not considered secure.

>> When the Swipe lock is enabled, you may see some start-up app icons on the Lock screen. Swipe an icon by dragging it with your finger, and then that app starts.

>> The Lock screen doesn't appear when the None screen lock is chosen.

>> The PIN and Password locks are required for certain tablet security settings, such as when you have a kid's account configured or you use the tablet to access a secure email system.

>> Biometric locks are available on some Tabs. These include a fingerprint lock, an iris scan, and facial recognition. See Chapter 21 for more details on setting and configuring screen locks.

More Accounts for Your Tab

The Galaxy Tab can be home to your various online incarnations, including your email accounts, online services, subscriptions, and other digital personas. I recommend adding those accounts to your tablet to continue the setup-and-configuration process.

With the tablet on and unlocked, follow these steps:

1. View the Apps screen.

Swipe the Home screen from bottom to top to view the Apps screen.

2. Open the Settings app.

You may have to swipe the Apps screen right or left to locate the Settings app.

After you tap the Settings icon, the Settings screen appears. It lists items for configuring and setting tablet options.

3. Choose Cloud and Accounts.

On some Tabs, tap the General tab.

4. **Select the Accounts category.**

You see any existing accounts, as shown in Figure 2-2, though you might see only your Google account.

Cloud and Accounts item

Add Account

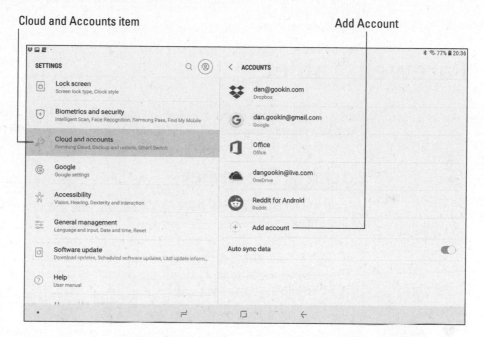

FIGURE 2-2:
Accounts in the
Settings app.

5. **Tap the Add Account item.**

6. **Select an account type from the list.**

For example, if you haven't yet added your Google account, choose Google.

Don't worry if you don't see the exact type of account you want to add. You may have to add an app before a specific account appears. Chapter 16 covers adding apps.

7. **Follow the directions on the screen to sign in to your account.**

Generally speaking, you sign in using an existing username and password. Some accounts may have an option that lets you create an account when you don't already have one.

Repeat these steps to continue adding accounts.

>> See Chapter 7 for specific information on adding email accounts to the Galaxy Tab.

>> Chapter 10 covers social networking on your tablet. Refer to that chapter for information on adding Facebook and Twitter accounts.

>> The accounts you add are your own. If you need to add another user to the tablet, another person who uses the same tablet, see Chapter 21 for information.

Farewell, Tablet

I know of three ways to say goodbye to your Galaxy tablet, and only one of them involves a steamroller. The other methods are documented in this section.

Locking the tablet

To lock the tablet, press the Power Lock button. The touchscreen goes dark; the tablet is locked.

REMEMBER

>> The Tab continues to work while it's locked; it receives email, can play music, and signals alerts. While it's locked, the tablet doesn't use as much power as it would with the display on.

>> Your tablet will spend most of its time locked.

>> Locking doesn't turn off the tablet.

>> Any timers or alarms you set still activate when the tablet is locked. See Chapter 15 for information on setting timers and alarms.

>> To unlock the tablet, press and release the Power Lock button. See the section "Unlocking the tablet," earlier in this chapter.

>> Refer to Chapter 20 for information on setting the automatic timeout value for the Lock screen.

Turning off your Galaxy Tab

To turn off the tablet, heed these steps:

1. Press and hold down the Power Lock button.

You see the Device Options menu, shown in Figure 2-3.

If you chicken out and don't want to turn off the tablet, tap the Back navigation icon to dismiss the Device Options menu.

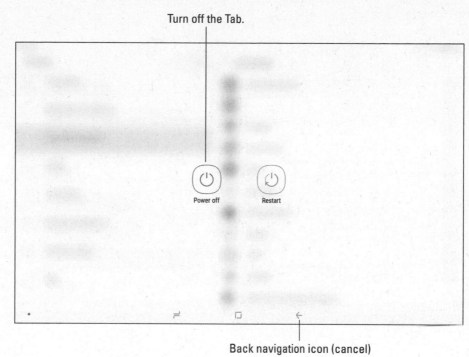

Turn off the Tab.

Power off

Restart

FIGURE 2-3:
The Device
Options menu.

Back navigation icon (cancel)

2. **Choose the Power Off item.**

3. **Confirm your choice: Tap the button again or tap OK.**

The tablet turns itself off.

If you change your mind, tap the Back navigation icon. (Refer to Figure 2-3.)

The tablet doesn't run when it's off, so it doesn't remind you of appointments, collect email, or let you hear any alarms you've set.

Neither is the tablet angry with you for turning it off, though you may sense some resentment when you turn it on again.

Restarting the tablet

When you must turn the tablet off and then turn it on again, choose Restart from the Device Options menu. (Refer to Figure 2-3.) A restart often fixes minor tablet woes.

>> You rarely need to restart the Galaxy Tab.

>> See Chapter 23 for information on tablet troubleshooting.

Chapter **3**

Galactic Procedures

Those computers in the Batcave back in the 1960's TV show *Batman* had lots of blinking lights. They showed how powerful the devices were, always busy and always thinking. More lights and knobs showed power.

Today, Batman's Batcave could get by with a single Galaxy Tab. Despite its lack of blinking lights and knobs, it's a powerful gizmo that would help fight crime and issue swift justice. Such things happen only when you know how to properly work the Tab's interface.

Basic Operations

To use the Galaxy Tab, you must work the touchscreen. This process goes against everything you learned when your folks insisted that you never touch the TV.

Touching the touchscreen

You can use one or two fingers, or you can use the tip of your big toe sticking out of your sock. It doesn't matter how, but touch the screen you must.

Here are some of the common ways to manipulate the touchscreen:

Tap: The basic touchscreen maneuver is to touch it. You tap an object, an icon, a control, a menu item, a doodad, and so on. The tap operation is similar to a mouse-click on a computer. It may also be referred to as a *touch* or a *press*.

Double-tap: Touch the screen twice in the same location. Double-tapping can be used to zoom in on an image or a map, but it can also zoom out. Because of the double-tap's dual nature, I recommend instead using the pinch or spread operation to zoom.

Long-press: Touch part of the screen and keep your finger down. Depending on what you're doing, a pop-up menu may appear, or the item you're long-pressing may get "picked up" so that you can move it around. A long-press might also be referred to as "touch and hold down" in the documentation.

Swipe: To swipe, you touch your finger on one spot and then move your finger to another spot. Swipes can go up, down, left, or right; the touchscreen content moves in the direction in which you swipe your finger. A swipe can be fast or slow. It's also called a *flick* or a *slide*.

Drag: A combination of long-press and then swipe, the drag operation moves items on the screen.

Pinch: A pinch involves two fingers, which start out separated and then are brought together. The effect is used to *zoom out*, to reduce the size of an image or see more of a map.

Spread: The opposite of pinch is spread. You start out with your fingers together and then spread them. The spread is used to *zoom in*, to enlarge an image or see more detail on a map.

Rotate: A few apps let you rotate an image on the screen by touching with two fingers and twisting them around a center point. Think of turning a combination lock on a safe to best understand the rotate operation.

REMEMBER

You can't manipulate the touchscreen while wearing gloves unless they're gloves designed for using electronic touchscreens, such as the gloves that Batman wears.

Changing the orientation

Your Galaxy Tab features a gizmo called an *accelerometer*. It determines in which direction the tablet is pointed or whether you've reoriented the device from an upright position to a horizontal one, or even upside down. That way, the information on the touchscreen always appears upright, no matter how you hold the Tab.

To demonstrate how the tablet orients itself, rotate the device clockwise or counterclockwise. Most apps change their orientation to match however you've turned the tablet. (See Figure 3-1.)

Horizontal orientation

Vertical orientation

The rotation feature may not work for all apps, especially games, which may present themselves in one orientation only.

TIP

>> The onscreen keyboard is more usable when the tablet is in its horizontal orientation. See Chapter 4.

>> You can lock the orientation if the rotating screen bothers you. See the "Making Quick Settings" section, later in this chapter.

>> When docked with the book cover keyboard, or when using DeX, the Tab orients itself horizontally and stays that way. See Chapter 5.

>> A nifty application for demonstrating the accelerometer is the game Labyrinth. It can be purchased at the Google Play Store, or the free version, Labyrinth Lite, can be downloaded. See Chapter 16 for more information about the Google Play Store.

Using the navigation icons

At the bottom of the touchscreen dwell three symbols. These are the navigation icons, and they help get you around as you use your Galaxy tablet.

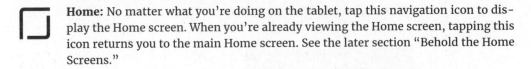 **Home:** No matter what you're doing on the tablet, tap this navigation icon to display the Home screen. When you're already viewing the Home screen, tapping this icon returns you to the main Home screen. See the later section "Behold the Home Screens."

Back: The Back navigation icon serves several purposes, all of which fit neatly under the concept of "back." Tap this icon to return to a previous page, dismiss an onscreen menu, close a window, hide the onscreen keyboard, and so on.

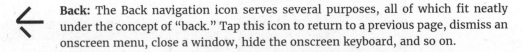 **Recent:** Tapping the Recent navigation icon displays the Overview. See the later section "Switching between running apps" for details.

Older Galaxy Tabs use different icons for these buttons. The Home button might also by a physical button you press.

Setting the volume

Sometimes the sound level is too loud. Sometimes it's too soft. And rarely, it's just right. Finding that just-right level is the job of the Volume key, which clings to the edge of the Galaxy Tab.

If the Volume key is on top of the tablet, press the left part of the key to increase the volume and the right part to decrease the volume. If the Volume key is on the side of the tablet, press the top part to make the volume louder and the bottom part to make the volume softer.

As you press the Volume key, a graphic appears on the touchscreen to illustrate the relative volume level, as shown in Figure 3-2.

Tap the chevron, shown in Figure 3-2, to see detailed volume controls. You can individually set the volume for notifications, media, and system sounds, as shown in the expanded onscreen volume control: Swipe the dot left or right to set the volume.

>> *Notifications* are alerts to new items, such as incoming email, a chat request, or an appointment reminder.

>> *Media* includes music that plays, sound from a video, and noise in a video game.

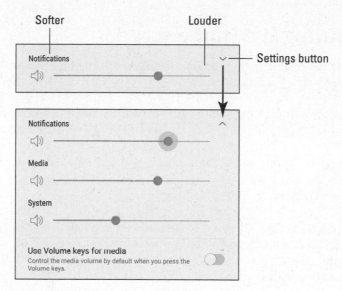

Softer   Louder

Settings button

FIGURE 3-2:
Setting the
volume.

>> *System* sounds are the noises made by the onscreen keyboard, warnings, alarms, and similar audio.

>> When the volume is set all the way down, the tablet is silenced and placed in vibration mode. (Not every tablet features vibration mode.)

>> You can also use the Sound Quick Action to adjust the volume. See the later section "Making Quick Settings."

>> The Settings app is the primary location for setting sounds. Refer to Chapter 20 for details.

>> The Volume key works even when the tablet is locked. That means you need not unlock the device to adjust the volume while you're listening to music.

REMEMBER

Behold the Home Screens

The main base from which you begin exploration of your Galaxy Tab is the *Home* screen. It's the first thing you see after unlocking the tablet, and the place you go to whenever you quit an app.

REMEMBER

To view the Home screen at any time, tap the Home navigation icon, located at the bottom of the touchscreen.

Touring the Home screen

Many interesting items festoon the Galaxy Tab's Home screen, as illustrated in Figure 3-3.

I recommend that you familiarize yourself with the following items and terms when using the Home screen:

Status bar: The top part of the screen, this area shows notification icons and status icons. The status bar may disappear, in which case a quick swipe downward from the top of the screen redisplays it.

Notification icons: These icons come and go, depending on what happens in your digital life. Notification icons appear whenever you receive new email messages or have pending appointments. The later section "Reviewing notifications," describes how to deal with notifications.

Status icons: These icons represent the tablet's current condition, such as the type of connected network, signal strength, battery status, and Bluetooth connection.

App launcher icons: The meat of the meal on the Home screen plate, app (application) launcher icons are where the action takes place. Tap a launcher icon to open (launch) an app.

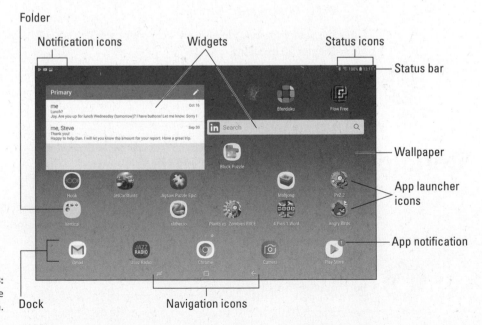

FIGURE 3-3: The Home screen.

App notifications: These tiny number bubbles affix themselves to app launcher icons. Their value represents pending actions, unread email, waiting messages, and other issues that require your attention.

Widgets: A widget is a window through which you view information, control the tablet, access features, or do something purely amusing.

Folders: Tap a folder to see a pop-up window that lists the apps stored inside. Folders allow you to organize apps as well as put more app launchers on the Home screen than would otherwise fit. See Chapter 19 for more information on folders.

Wallpaper: The background image you see on the Home screen is the wallpaper. It can be changed, as described in Chapter 20.

The Dock: This row of launchers stays consistent despite whichever Home screen page you're viewing. It's home to apps you use most frequently.

Navigation icons: These controls are almost always available. When you don't see them, swipe the screen from the top downward, and they appear. Refer to the earlier section "Using the navigation icons."

Ensure that you recognize the various parts of the Home screen and their names. These terms are used throughout this book and in whatever other scant Galaxy Tab documentation exists.

TIP

The Home screen is customizable. You can add and remove launchers, widgets, and folders and even change wallpaper (background) images. See Chapter 20 for more information.

Reviewing notifications

Notifications appear as icons at the top left of the Home screen. (Refer to Figure 3-5.) To see the details, pull down the notifications shade: Swipe the screen downward from the tippy-top. The notifications shade is illustrated in Figure 3-4.

Tap a notification to deal with it. What happens next depends on the notification, but most often the app that generated the notification appears. You might also be given the opportunity to deal with whatever caused the notification, such as a calendar appointment.

To dismiss an individual notification, swipe it to the right or left. To dismiss all notifications, tap the CLEAR button. Some ongoing notifications, such as a notification describing a USB connection, cannot be dismissed.

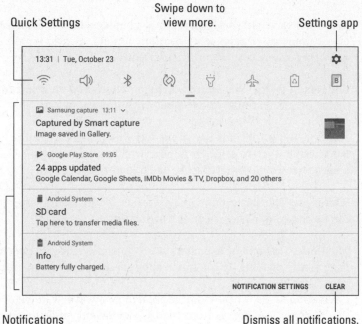

Quick Settings — Swipe down to view more. — Settings app

13:31 | Tue, October 23

Samsung capture 13:11
Captured by Smart capture
Image saved in Gallery.

Google Play Store 09:05
24 apps updated
Google Calendar, Google Sheets, IMDb Movies & TV, Dropbox, and 20 others

Android System
SD card
Tap here to transfer media files.

Android System
Info
Battery fully charged.

NOTIFICATION SETTINGS   CLEAR

FIGURE 3-4:
The notifications panel. — Notifications — Dismiss all notifications.

To hide the notifications shade, swipe it up to the top of the screen or tap the Back navigation icon.

>> Dismissing some notifications doesn't prevent them from appearing again in the future. For example, notifications to update apps continue to appear, as do calendar reminders.

>> Some apps, such as Facebook and Twitter, don't display notifications unless you're logged in. See Chapter 10.

>> The Tab plays a notification ringtone whenever a new notification floats in. See Chapter 20 for information on choosing which sound plays.

Making Quick Settings

Many common settings and features for your Galaxy Tab can be found atop the notifications panel. These Quick Settings appear as large icons. (Refer to Figure 3-4).

To activate a setting, tap its icon. When the setting is on, it appears highlighted. Tap a highlighted setting to turn it off. For example, tap the Sound Quick Setting to cycle between sound on, mute, or vibrate-only modes.

Swipe the Quick Settings downward to view more icons as well as see descriptions of which tablet features each icon controls.

Various Quick Settings are covered throughout this book. Generally speaking, any tablet feature that can be turned on or off — such as Wi-Fi, Bluetooth, Airplane mode, or Sound — can be accessed quickly as a Quick Setting.

All About Those Apps

The primary thing you do on the Home screen is run apps, which appear as app launcher icons. Knowing how to start, or *launch,* an app is the key to getting the most from your Galaxy Tab.

>> *App* is short for *app*lication. It's another word for *program* or *software.*

>> Also see Chapter 24 for information on running apps by using the Multi Window feature.

Starting an app

To start an app, tap its launcher. The app starts.

You can also start an app found in a Home screen folder: Tap to open the folder, and then tap a launcher to start that app.

Quitting an app

Unlike on a computer, you need not quit apps on your Galaxy Tab. To leave an app, tap the Home navigation icon to return to the Home screen. You can keep tapping the Back navigation icon to back out of an app. Or you can tap the Recent navigation icon to switch to another running app.

>> A handful of apps do feature a Quit action or Exit action, but for the most part, don't look to quit an app on your Tab.

>> If necessary, the Android operating system shuts down apps you haven't used in a while. You can directly stop apps running amok, as described in Chapter 19.

Working with widgets

Like apps, widgets appear on the Home screen. To use a widget, tap it. What happens after that depends on the widget and what it does.

For example, the YouTube widget lets you peruse videos. The Calendar widget shows a preview of your upcoming schedule. A Twitter widget may display recent tweets. Other widgets do interesting things, display useful information, or give you access to the tablet's settings or features.

See Chapter 19 for details on working with widgets on the Home screen.

Visiting the Apps screen

The launcher icons you see on the Home screen don't represent all the apps on your tablet. To view all installed apps, you must visit the Apps screen: Swipe the Home screen from bottom to top. You see the first page of the Apps screen, as shown in Figure 3-5.

Similar to the Home screen, the Apps screen has several pages of apps. An index appears at the bottom of the screen. (Refer to Figure 3-5.) Swipe the screen left or right to view the various pages.

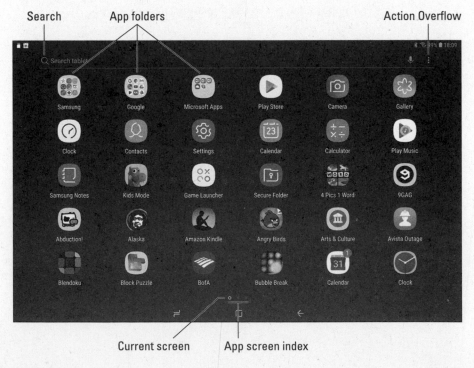

FIGURE 3-5:
The Apps screen.

To start an app from the Apps screen, tap its icon. The app starts.

Like the Home screen, the Apps screen contains app folders. Tap a folder to view its contents.

>> Consider placing launcher icons on the Home screen for those apps you use most often. See Chapter 19.

>> See Chapter 19 also for information on creating Apps screen folders.

Switching between running apps

The apps you run on your Galaxy Tab don't quit when you set them aside. For the most part, they stay running. To switch between running apps, or to any app you've recently opened, tap the Recent navigation icon, shown in the margin. You see the Overview, similar to what's shown in Figure 3-6.

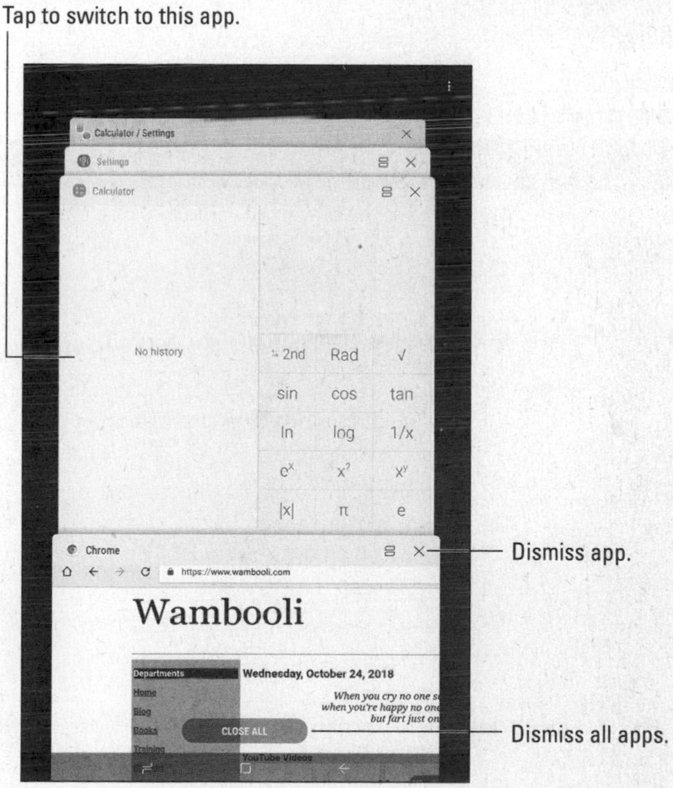

Tap to switch to this app.

— Dismiss app.

— Dismiss all apps.

FIGURE 3-6:
Recently used
apps on the
Overview.

Choose an app from the Overview to switch to it.

REMEMBER

» You can remove an app from the Overview by swiping it or left or right. This is almost the same thing as quitting an app. Almost.

» To clear the Overview, tap the CLOSE ALL button.

» Apps on the Galaxy Tab lack a Quit action or Exit action. They keep running, so using the Overview is a great way to switch between running apps.

» Also remember that the Android operating system may shut down apps that haven't received attention for a while. Don't be surprised if you see an app missing from the Overview. If so, just start it up again as you normally would.

Recognizing common icons

In additional to the navigation icons, various other icons appear while you use your Galaxy Tab. These icons serve common functions in your apps as well as in the Android operating system. Table 3-1 lists the most common icons and their functions.

TABLE 3-1 **Common Icons**

Icon	Name	What It Does
⋮	Action Overflow	Displays a menu or a list of commands (actions).
✚	Add	Adds or creates a new item. The plus symbol (+) may be used with other symbols, depending on the app.
✕	Close	Closes a window or clears text from an input field.
🗑	Delete	Removes one or more items from a list or deletes a message.
🎤	Dictation	Lets you use your voice to dictate text.
✓	Done	Dismisses an action bar, such as the text-editing action bar.

Icon	Name	What It Does
	Edit	Lets you edit an item, add text, or fill in fields.
	Favorite	Flags a favorite item, such as a contact or a web page.
	Refresh	Fetches new information or reloads.
	Search	Searches the tablet or the Internet for some tidbit of information.
	Settings	Adjusts options for an app.
	Share	Shares information stored on the tablet via email or social networking or another Internet services.
	Side Menu	Displays the navigation drawer, listing actions and options for an app.

Various sections throughout this book give examples of using the icons. Their images appear in the book's margins where relevant.

Other common symbols are used on icons in various apps. For example, the standard Play and Pause icons are used as well.

IN THIS CHAPTER

» **Using the onscreen keyboard**

» **Accessing special characters**

» **Creating text by using the keyboard swipe**

» **Dictating text with voice input**

» **Editing text**

» **Selecting, cutting, copying, and pasting text**

Chapter **4**

Text to Type and Edit

The notion of a keyboard adds too many buttons to an otherwise sleek and mobile device like your Galaxy Tab. Even so, text input is still required. Though you most likely won't use your Galactic tablet to write a novel, you are required to write text. To fulfill that function, and to help you edit and hone your text, you use something called the onscreen keyboard.

This Is a Keyboard?

When text input is required, the onscreen keyboard, shown in Figure 4-1, reveals itself on the bottom half of the screen.

The Enter key changes its look depending on what you're typing. Four variations are shown in Figure 4-1. Here's what each one does:

» **Enter:** Just like the Enter or Return key on a computer keyboard, this key ends a paragraph of text. It's used mostly when filling in long stretches of text or when multiline input is needed.

» **Go:** This action key directs an app to do something, such as visit a web page or initiate a search.

» **Next:** This key appears when you're typing information in multiple fields. Touch this key to switch from one field to the next, such as when typing a username and a password.

» **Done:** This key appears when you have finished typing text in the final field and are ready to submit the information.

The large key at the bottom center of the onscreen keyboard is the Space key. To the right of the Space key, you find the .com key, which displays quick shortcuts for typing web page and email addresses. Farther right are two triangle keys used to move the cursor.

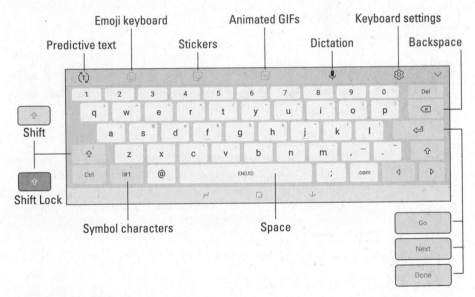

FIGURE 4-1:
The onscreen keyboard.

The Enter key changes its look depending on what you're typing. Four variations are shown in Figure 4-1. Here's what each one does:

» **Enter:** Just like the Enter or Return key on a computer keyboard, this key ends a paragraph of text. It's used mostly when filling in long stretches of text or when multiline input is needed.

» **Go:** This action key directs an app to do something, such as visit a web page or initiate a search.

>> **Next:** This key appears when you're typing information in multiple fields. Touch this key to switch from one field to the next, such as when typing a username and a password.

>> **Done:** This key appears when you have finished typing text in the final field and are ready to submit the information.

The large key at the bottom center of the onscreen keyboard is the Space key. To the right of the Space key, you find the .com key, which displays quick shortcuts for typing web page and email addresses. Farther right are two triangle keys used to move the cursor.

Above the keyboard is an icon bar that changes the keyboard's look. The far left icon switches between text typing suggestions and various other keyboards: emojis, stickers (larger images), animated GIFs, dictation (voice input), and the keyboard settings screen.

>> To summon the onscreen keyboard, touch any text field or spot on the screen where typing is permitted.

>> To dismiss the onscreen keyboard, tap the Back navigation icon.

>> The onscreen keyboard reorients itself when you rotate the tablet. The onscreen keyboard's horizontal orientation is the easiest to use.

TIP

>> If you pine for a real keyboard, one that exists in the fourth dimension, you're not out of luck. You can use any Bluetooth keyboard with the Tab. Refer to Chapter 17 for details on connecting Bluetooth devices.

>> Chapter 5 covers the Samsung book cover keyboard, which is the official "real" keyboard.

REMEMBER

>> When a real keyboard is connected to the Tab, the onscreen keyboard doesn't appear.

The Old Hunt-and-Peck

The purpose of the onscreen keyboard is to type, to generate text or input for the tablet. For the most part, using the keyboard makes sense. For the rest of the parts that don't make sense, turn to this section.

Typing one character at a time

Using the onscreen keyboard to type is simple: Tap a letter to produce the character. The keyboard makes a pleasant clicking sound as you type, and the tablet may
vibrate slightly.

>> To type in all caps, tap the Shift key twice. Tap the Shift key again to return to
normal typing.

>> Above all, it helps to type slowly as you get used to the onscreen keyboard.

>> A blinking cursor on the touchscreen shows where new text appears, which is
similar to how text input works on a computer.

>> When you make a mistake, tap the Backspace key to back up and erase. Use
the Del (delete) key to remove a character to the right of the cursor.

>> When you type a password, each character appears briefly and is then
replaced by a black dot, for security reasons.

Accessing special characters

To access additional characters, tap the !#1 key on the onscreen keyboard. You see
one of two additional keyboard layouts, shown in Figure 4-2.

Tap the 1/2 or 2/2 key on either side to switch between the symbol keyboards,
illustrated in Figure 4-2.

To return to the standard alpha keyboard (refer to Figure 4-1), tap the ABC key.

TIP

You can access special character keys from the main alphabetic keyboard,
provided you know a secret: *Long-press* (touch and hold down) a key. When you
do, you see a pop-up palette of additional characters, similar to the ones shown
for the A key in Figure 4-3.

To access these characters, follow these steps:

1. **Long-press a key.**

   If a pop-up palette of alternative characters doesn't appear, the letter you
   pressed doesn't support this feature.

2. **Drag your finger up to the symbol you want to type.**

3. **Lift your finger to produce that character.**

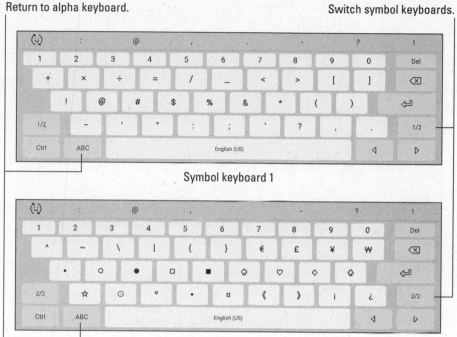

Return to alpha keyboard.

Switch symbol keyboards.

Symbol keyboard 1

Symbol keyboard 2

FIGURE 4-2:
Number and
symbol
keyboards.

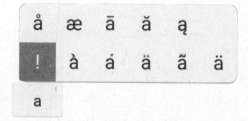

FIGURE 4-3:
Special
symbol pop-up
palette thing.

If you make a mistake, you can't back out of the pop-up palette. In that case, just type the incorrect character, and then tap the Backspace key to erase it.

Typing quickly by using predictive text

As you type, you may see a selection of word suggestions just above the keyboard. That's the tablet's Predictive Text feature, which you can use to greatly accelerate your typing.

In Figure 4-4, I typed the word *I*. The keyboard then suggested the words *don't*, *think*, and *am*. Each of these is a logical choice for the next word after *I*. Additional choices are viewed by tapping the chevron, as illustrated in the figure. Tap one of the suggested words to insert it in the text.

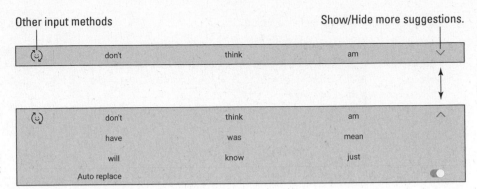

FIGURE 4-4:
Predictive text
in action.

When the desired word doesn't appear, continue typing: The Predictive Text feature begins making suggestions based on what you've typed so far. Tap the desired word when it appears.

If you don't see the word *suggestions*, tap the Predictive Text icon, shown in the margin.

To ensure that the Predictive Text has been activated on your Tab, follow these steps:

1. Tap the Keyboard Settings icon above the onscreen keyboard.

If you don't see this icon, tap the Other Input Methods icon, shown in the margin and illustrated in Figure 4-4. Refer to Figure 4-1 for the Keyboard Settings icon's location.

2. Choose Smart Typing.

3. Ensure that the Master Control icon next to the Predictive Text option is on.

4. Tap the Back button a few times to return to your typing.

Likewise, if you find predictive text boring and predictable, disable it by repeating these steps but turning off the master control in Step 3.

Adding keyboard swipe

If you're really after typing speed, use the onscreen keyboard's swipe feature. It allows you to type words by swiping your finger over the keyboard, like mad scribbling but with a positive result. Figure 4-5 illustrates how the word *hello* is typed in this manner.

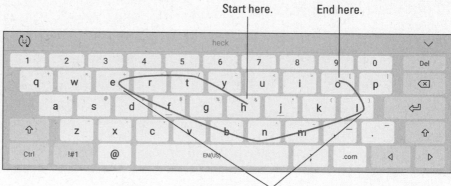

Start here.   End here.

Keep your finger down as you drag over the letters.

FIGURE 4-5:
Using keyboard
swipe to
type *hello*.

Keyboard swipe is enabled by default. If not, or to disable this feature, follow these steps:

1. Tap the Keyboard Settings icon.

The icon is labeled in Figure 4-1. If you don't see the icon, tap the Other Input Methods icon, shown in the margin.

2. Choose Smart Typing.

3. On the right side of the screen, choose Keyboard Swipe Controls.

4. Ensure that Swipe to Type is selected.

The keyboard swipe feature is disabled for typing a password or when using specific apps on the tablet.

Google Voice Typing

The Galaxy Tab has the amazing capability to interpret your utterances as text. It works almost as well as computer dictation in science fiction movies, though I can't seem to find the command to destroy the planet Alderaan.

Dictating text

To talk to your tablet, tap the Dictation icon, shown in the margin. This icon's location is referenced earlier, in Figure 4-1. When the tablet is ready to listen, a special window appears at the bottom of the screen, similar to what's shown in Figure 4-6. Dictate some text.

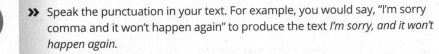

Close dictation.

Tap to pause

Google

FIGURE 4-6:
Google Voice
typing.

Dictation settings

Delete word.

As you speak, the Microphone icon flashes. The flashing doesn't mean that the tablet is embarrassed by what you're saying. No, the flashing merely indicates that your words are being digested, soon to appear as text.

To pause, touch the Tap to Pause text on the screen. To use the keyboard, tap the X Close Dictation icon. Or, to continue dictation, touch the Tap to Speak text.

REMEMBER

» The better your diction, the better the results.

» You can't use dictation to edit text. Text editing still takes place on the touchscreen, as described in the later section "Text Editing."

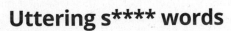

TIP

» Speak the punctuation in your text. For example, you would say, "I'm sorry comma and it won't happen again" to produce the text *I'm sorry, and it won't happen again.*

» Common punctuation you can dictate includes the comma, period, exclamation point, question mark, colon, and new line (to start text on the next line).

» You can't dictate capital letters. If you're a stickler for such things, you must go back and edit the text.

» Dictation may not work without an Internet connection.

Uttering s**** words

WARNING

The Galaxy Tab features a voice censor. Any naughty words you might utter are replaced; the first letter appears on the screen, followed by the appropriate number of asterisks.

For example, if *spatula* were a blue word and you uttered *spatula* when dictating text, the dictation feature would place *s******* on the screen rather than the word *spatula.*

Yeah, I know: silly. Or s****.

The tablet knows a lot of blue terms, including the infamous "Seven Words You Can Never Say on Television," but apparently the terms *crap* and *damn* are fine. Don't ask me how much time I spent researching this topic.

See Chapter 24 if you want the tablet to take naughty dictation.

Text Editing

You'll probably do more text editing on your Galaxy Tab than you realize. That editing includes the basic stuff, such as spiffing up typos and adding a period here or there as well as complex editing involving cut, copy, and paste. The concepts are the same as you find on a computer, but the process can be daunting without a keyboard and mouse.

Moving the cursor

The first part of editing text is to move the cursor to the right spot. The *cursor* is that blinking vertical line where text appears. On most computing devices, you move the cursor by using a pointing device. Your tablet has no pointing device, but you do: your finger.

To move the cursor, touch the spot on the text where you want the cursor to appear. To help your precision, a cursor tab appears below the text, as shown in the margin. Move that tab with your finger to move the cursor in the text.

For fine adjustments, use the left-right triangle keys on the keyboard to move the cursor back and forth in 1-character increments.

TIP

After you move the cursor, you can continue to type, use the Backspace key to back up and erase, tap the Del key to erase the character to the right, or paste text copied from elsewhere.

Selecting text

Selecting text on the Galaxy Tab works like selecting text in a word processor: You mark the start and end of a block. A block of text appears highlighted on the screen. How you get there, however, can be a mystery — until now!

Start selecting by long-pressing the text or double-tapping a word. Upon success, you see a chunk of text selected, as shown in Figure 4-7.

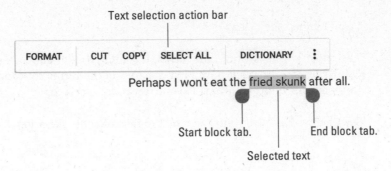

FIGURE 4-7:
Text is selected.

Drag the start and end markers around the touchscreen to define the selected text.

When text is selected, an action bar appears, as illustrated in Figure 4-7. It lists common commands for dealing with the text, including Cut, Copy, and Select All. Other commands may also appear, depending on the app or context of the text. See the later section "Cutting, copying, and pasting."

TIP

>> Selecting text on a web page works the same as selecting text in any other app. The big difference is that text can only be copied from the web page, not cut or deleted.

>> You can select all text by tapping Ctrl+A on the onscreen keyboard: Long-press the Ctrl (control) key and tap the A key.

>> To cancel the selection, tap outside the selected block.

Cutting, copying, and pasting

Selected text is primed for cutting or copying, which works just like it does in your favorite word processor. After you select the text, choose the proper command from the text selection action bar, as illustrated in Figure 4-7:

Copy: Tap COPY to copy the selected text. Or, you can long-press the onscreen keyboard's Ctrl key and tap the C key to copy.

Cut: Tap CUT to cut the selected text. Or, you can long-press the Ctrl key and tap the X key to cut.

Cut or copied text is stored in the Galaxy Tab's clipboard.

Paste: To paste any previously cut or copied text, move the cursor to the spot where you want the text pasted. Tap the Paste command button on the action bar, shown in Figure 4-8. If you don't see the action bar, tap the cursor tab and it appears.

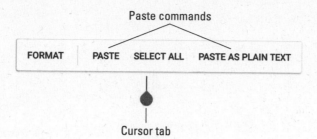

FIGURE 4-8:
Paste commands
on the action bar.

You can also paste by long-pressing the onscreen keyboard's Ctrl key and tapping the V key.

REMEMBER

>> You can paste text only in locations where text is allowed. Odds are good that whenever you see the onscreen keyboard, you can paste text.

>> Physical keyboards may sport the Ctrl key, which can also be used to copy, cut, or paste: Ctrl+C, Ctrl+X, and Ctrl+V, respectively.

Undoing and redoing mistakes

The Undo and Redo commands are popular with computer users worldwide. A real-life equivalent of Undo and Redo remains to be found, but the Galaxy Tab is happy to oblige:

>> Long-press the onscreen keyboard's Ctrl key and tap the X key to undo a previous action. This includes deleting text, moving text, and even typing new text.

>> Long-press the Ctrl key and tap the Y key to "undo the undo."

Chapter 5

Tab Toys and Peripherals

The Galaxy Tab is a marvelous gizmo all by itself. It does just about everything you need, but wait (as they say on those loud infomercials) — there's more! The S Pen allows for precise touchscreen interaction. The Samsung book cover keyboard provides an excellent way to prop up the tablet and offer a physical keyboard. It also works well with the DeX desktop environment, which offers another approach to using the Tab.

The Samsung Book Cover Keyboard and DeX

A great way to keep your Tab safe is to use a pouch or another carrying device, such as the book cover keyboard offered by Samsung. It keeps the tablet safe from casual damage, props it up for easy viewing, provides a physical keyboard for typing, and serves as an ideal peripheral for the DeX desktop.

» The book cover keyboard features an attachment for inserting the S Pen. Though handy, it's impractical. I recommend removing the S Pen holder and keeping the S Pen in your pocket or stored elsewhere.

» The book cover keyboard isn't a Bluetooth peripheral. It communicates directly with the Tab.

Connecting to the book cover keyboard

The Galaxy Tab S4 fits snugly into the book cover keyboard, which instantly recognizes the device's presence and starts the DeX desktop environment. Figure 5-1 illustrates the Tab S4 docked in the book cover keyboard and running DeX.

DeX desktop

FIGURE 5-1.
The book cover
keyboard.

Useless S Pen holder   Keyboard   S Pen

Removing the Tab from the book cover keyboard requires some ingenuity and effort. It's best to grab a top corner and pry the book cover keyboard back and away from the device to free it from the cover's clutches.

» The book cover keyboard lacks batteries, so it doesn't need to be charged. It does use the tablet's power, but not enough to raise power management concerns.

» The Tab is inserted only one way. The rear camera aligns with the hole on the back of the book cover keyboard; the Power/Lock key is on the top left as the tablet faces you.

>> You can use the Tab in the book cover keyboard with or without the DeX desktop. See the later section "Exiting from DeX" for details.

Activating DeX manually

Even if you don't have the book cover keyboard, you can direct your Tab to show the DeX desktop environment. Heed these directions:

1. **Open the Settings app.**

2. **Chose Advanced Features.**

3. **On the right side of the screen, by the item Samsung DeX, slide the master control to the On position.**

    DeX starts instantly.

See the later section "Exiting from DeX" for details on how to escape.

Exploring DeX

Upon inserting the Tab into the book cover keyboard, you may see the Samsung DeX desktop environment appear on the touchscreen. This environment replaces the Android interface that you're familiar with and that is documented throughout the rest of this book.

DeX is a desktop environment for the Galaxy Tab, similar to the desktop environment of Windows but running Android apps. If you're familiar with Android, you'll find DeX a strange land, but one that is geared toward productivity.

The DeX desktop is shown in Figure 5-2. Don't expect to find anything familiar from Android on the desktop; common features have new locations, as illustrated in the figure.

Apps

To start an app, tap the Apps Screen button in the lower left corner of the desktop. Choose an app to launch. You can also tap the Recent icon to select a recently opened app from the Overview.

To close an app, tap one of the Close buttons in its window.

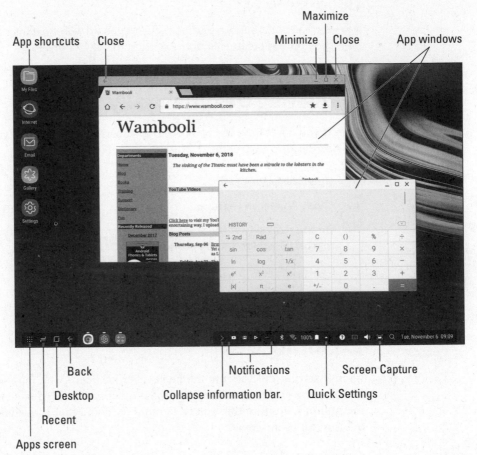

App shortcuts   Close   Minimize   Maximize   Close   App windows

Notifications   Screen Capture

Collapse information bar.   Quick Settings

Back

Desktop

Recent

FIGURE 5-2:
The DeX desktop.   Apps screen

Windows

DeX presents your apps in windows, such as those shown in Figure 5-2. As with a desktop operating system, the windows can be moved, resized, minimized, maximized, and closed. These actions work similarly on the Tab as they do in Windows or in any desktop environment.

Notifications

A few notification icons appear at the bottom of the DeX desktop, on the information bar in the lower right portion of the screen. Tap a notification to view its contents. Tap the Ellipsis button (the three dots) to view the notifications shade.

Quick Settings

Tap the upward-pointing triangle in the Status area of the information bar to view the Quick Settings. Refer to Figure 5-2 for this icon's location.

App shortcuts

The DeX desktop features app shortcuts, which are similar to launcher icons on the Android desktop. Five of them are shown on the left in Figure 5-2.

To add an app shortcut, visit the Apps screen and long-press the app you want to add. From the pop-up, choose Add Shortcut to Home.

To remove an app shortcut, long-press its icon and choose Remove Shortcut. Removing a shortcut doesn't uninstall the app.

TIP

>> Tap the Keyboard icon on the information bar to access the onscreen keyboard. One reason to pop up this keyboard is to access accented and other special characters not obviously available on the book cover keyboard.

>> You can also pop up the onscreen keyboard by tapping the Keyboard button on the book cover keyboard, shown in the margin. This trick works in both the DeX environment and standard Android.

>> To quickly access the Calendar app, tap the date-and-time in the lower right corner of the screen.

>> See the section "Disabling DeX" if you prefer that the DeX desktop not appear when you insert the Tab into the book cover keyboard.

Exiting from DeX

The DeX desktop environment doesn't deactivate when you pry the Tab free from the book cover keyboard. To end a DeX session, follow these steps:

1. Tap the Quick Settings icon on the information bar.

2. Tap the Samsung DeX icon.

The DeX session ends.

Any apps open in DeX remain open when you return to the Android interface; tap the Recent icon to switch to them.

Alas, the Samsung DeX icon isn't available from the standard Android interface. To manually activate DeX, refer to the earlier section "Activating DeX manually."

Disabling DeX

To prevent DeX from starting when the Tab is inserted into the book cover keyboard, follow these steps:

1. Open the Settings app.

2. Choose Advanced Features.

3. On the right side of the screen, choose Samsung DeX.

4. Next to the item Auto Start When Book Cover Keyboard Is Connected, slide the master control to the Off position.

S Pen Scribbling

Better than your finger, the S Pen can be used to scribble input on the Galaxy Tab. This digital stylus opens a constellation of opportunities for input and manipulation. Yes, it can do more than simply draw mustaches on pictures.

>> The S Pen comes with the Galaxy Tab S4.

>> Unlike other digital styluses, the S Pen doesn't need to be synced with the Tab, nor does it contain batteries.

Understanding the S Pen

The S Pen is about the size of a writing pen. It has a pointy end and a not-so-pointy end. The pointy end is the one you use to manipulate the Tab's touchscreen.

Near the front of the S Pen is a button, illustrated in Figure 5-3. Use this button to help the S Pen perform some of its fancier tricks, but be aware that the button is found on only one side of the S Pen. That means there's a right way and a wrong way to hold the thing.

You can use the S Pen at any time as a handy substitute for your finger. All touchscreen manipulations you can do with a single finger can be performed by using the S Pen.

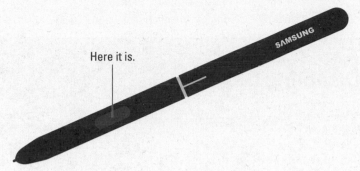

Here it is.

FIGURE 5-3:
Locating the S
Pen button.

The S Pen's location is mapped by a pointer on the touchscreen. The pointer appears as a small circle. To ensure that the pointer is active, follow these steps:

1. **Open the Settings app.**

2. **Choose Advanced Features.**

3. **On the right side of the screen, choose S Pen.**

4. **Ensure that the master control by the Pointer item is set to the On position.**

Using Air Command

Most of the fancy things you can do with the S Pen are easily accessed by tapping the Air Command icon, shown in the margin. This icon appears whenever you hover the mouse over the touchscreen. Tap the icon to see the Air Command display, illustrated in Figure 5-4.

The Icons arced on the screen (shown in Figure 5-4) can be rotated to view more, such as the Pen Up icon at the bottom of the figure. You can add more shortcuts by tapping the Add Shortcuts button.

Here are brief descriptions of the Air Command apps:

Create Note: Jot down a quick note, just as though you were scribbling on a pad of paper.

View All Notes: Open the Samsung Note app to review the notes you've scribbled. Tap the Add (Plus) icon to create a new note.

Smart Select: Use the S Pen to select a portion of the screen to save. Choose a selection tool to grab unusual shapes or GIF images.

S Pen Settings

Air Command icon

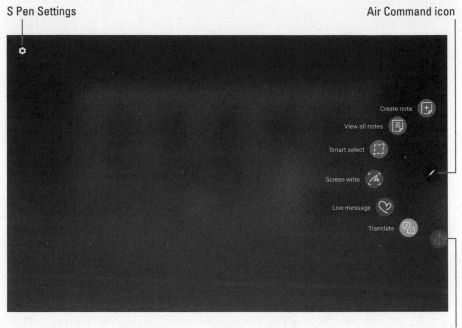

FIGURE 5-4:
Air Command.

Pen Up

Screen Write: The Screen Write command takes a picture of the screen — a *screen shot* — and then lets you use the S Pen to draw in it. The saved images can be accessed from the Gallery app.

Live Message: Create an animated image (a GIF file) using the S Pen to draw in various styles. The image saved can be viewed in the Gallery app.

Translate: Hold the S Pen over a word to translate it into the selected language.

PENUP: Choose this item to draw images and create graphics.

Many of these apps can be accessed directly from the Apps screen.

2

Tab
Communications

IN THIS PART . . .

Understand contacts and their options.

Work with email on your Tab.

Connect with text chat, video chat, and phone calls.

Explore on the web.

Discover your digital social life.

Chapter **6**

All Your Friends in the Galaxy

One of the Galaxy Tab's many duties is as a communications device. You can send and receive email, entertain your friends on social networking, or text and chat by using a variety of apps. The common theme is communicating with people. Therefore, it makes sense that your Tab features an app full of people you know or with whom you make frequent contact.

 The Galaxy Tab features two Contacts apps: one from Samsung and the other from Google. They both perform similar duties, though this chapter covers Samsung's version of the app, identified by the icon shown in the margin.

Meet the Tab's Address Book

The people you know — specifically, those associated with your various online accounts — are accessed by using the Contacts app on your Galaxy Tab. It pulls in contacts from your Gmail account, plus other accounts you've added to the tablet.

You can also manually add contacts. No matter how the people you know get there, the Contacts app is the place to look for them.

>> Many apps use contact information from the Contacts app, including Gmail and Hangouts as well as any app that lets you share information such as photographs or videos.

>> Information from your social networking apps is also coordinated with the Contacts app. See Chapter 10 for more information on using the tablet as your social networking hub.

Using the Contacts app

To peruse your tablet's address book, open the Contacts app. It can be found on the Apps screen, or you may find its launcher icon on the Home screen.

Figure 6-1 illustrates important parts of the Contacts app. Use the index (on the left side of the screen) to swiftly swipe through the list, or tap a letter to view contacts sorted by that letter. Tap a contact to view details, as shown on the right in Figure 6-1.

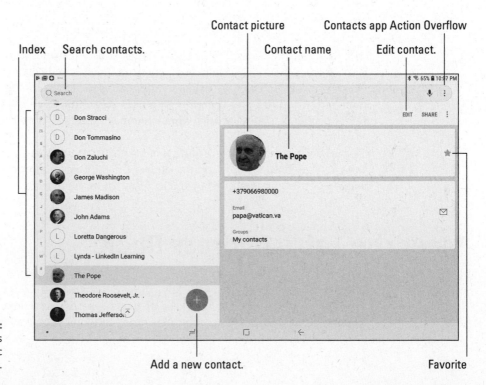

FIGURE 6-1: Your tablet's electronic address book.

The list of activities you can do with a contact depends on the information shown and the apps installed on your Tab. Here are some common activities:

Place a phone call: The Galaxy Tab is not a phone, but if you install the Hangouts Dialer or a similar app, you can use the phone information to place a call. See Chapter 8 for details.

Send email: Tap the contact's email address to compose an email message. When the contact has more than one email address, you can choose to which one you want to send the message. Chapter 7 covers email.

View address: When the contact lists a home or business address, you can tap that item to launch the Maps app to view the address. You can then get directions, look at the place using the Street View tool, or do any number of interesting things, as covered in Chapter 11.

Some tidbits of information that show up for a contact don't have an associated action. For example, the tablet won't sing "Happy Birthday" when you touch a contact's birthday information.

>> Not every contact has a picture, and the picture can come from a number of sources (Gmail or Facebook, for example). See the section "Taking a picture of a contact."

>> Also see the later section "Joining identical contacts" for information on how to deal with duplicate entries for the same person.

Sorting your contacts

Perhaps you like the address book sorted by last name, but with the first name first. Or, perhaps you want to see everyone last name first, but want them sorted by first name. Whatever the case, adjust the sort order by heeding these directions in the Contacts app:

1. Tap the Action Overflow icon.

Use the Action Overflow at the end of the Search box, as illustrated in Figure 6-1.

2. Choose Settings.

3. Choose Sort By.

4. **Select First Name or Last Name, depending on how you want the list sorted.**

5. **Choose Name Format.**

6. **Select First Last or Last First to direct the app to display the names in the given manner.**

The Contacts app normally displays your address book with first name first, sorted by first name.

Searching contacts

It's easy to find a contact by swiping the screen. It's easier to use the index to jump to a specific letter. When you have zillions of contacts, the best approach is to use the Search text box, shown in Figure 6-1.

Tap the Search text box. Use the onscreen keyboard to start typing a name. As you type, the list of contacts narrows until the exact person you're looking for is found.

Tap the X (Cancel) button in the Search text box to clear the search.

REMEMBER

No, there's no correlation between the number of contacts you have and how popular you are in real life.

Add More Friends

Having friends is great. Having more friends is better. Keeping all those friends as entries in Contacts is best.

>> Contacts are associated with your various online accounts and services. For example, your Google account plays host to all your Gmail contacts as well as new contacts you create.

>> If you use Yahoo! as your primary email account, create new contacts and associate them with that account. The next section offers details.

Creating a contact from scratch

Sometimes it's necessary to create a contact when you actually meet another human being in the real world, or maybe you finally got around to transferring information to the Tab from your old paper address book. In either instance, you have information to input, and it starts like this:

1. **Tap the Add Contact icon in the Contacts app.**

2. **Choose your Google account.**

   Your Google account is listed atop the new contact card. If not, tap that item and choose your Google account or whatever account you want to associate the contact with, such as your Yahoo! account.

   Do not choose the Tablet account item. When you do, the contact information is saved only on your Galaxy Tab. It isn't synchronized with the Internet or any other Android devices.

3. **Fill in information about the contact as best you can.**

   Fill in the text fields with the information you know: name, phone number, and type (mobile or work, for example), email address, and whatever other information you have.

4. **Tap the View More button to add fields, including Website.**

5. **Tap the SAVE button to add the contact.**

Providing that you followed my advice in Step 2, the new contact is automatically synced with your Google account. That's one beauty of the Android operating system used by the Galaxy Tab: You have no need to duplicate your efforts; contacts you create on the tablet are instantly updated with your Google account on the Internet.

Creating a contact from an email message

Perhaps one of the easiest ways to build up the Tab's address book is to create a contact from an email message. Follow these steps when you receive a message from someone not already in the address book:

1. **Tap the icon by the contact's name.**

   The Gmail app uses a letter icon for unknown contacts, such as the R shown in the margin. Upon successfully tapping the icon, you see an info card.

2. **Tap the Action Overflow on the info card.**

3. **Choose Add to Contacts.**

4. **Tap the Create Contact button to build a new contact, or, if the email is from someone whose name is already in the address book, choose a name to add the email address to that existing contact.**

5. **Ensure that your Google account is chosen for saving the contact.**

If not, choose Google Contact. Do not choose Tablet. Refer to the preceding section for my reason why Google is a good choice and Tablet is a poor choice.

6. **Fill in the contact's information.**

The email address is already supplied for you — a bonus! Even if you don't know the rest of the info, you're still creating a contact. You can always add more details later; see the later section "Editing contact information."

7. **Tap the SAVE button to add the contact.**

Grabbing contacts from your social networking sites

You can pour your whole gang of friends and followers from your social networking sites into the tablet. The operation is automatic: Add the social networking site's app to the tablet's inventory of apps as described in Chapter 10. At that time, you're prompted to sync the contacts or the apps are added instantly to the Contacts app's address book.

Importing contacts from a computer

You may be one of the few computer users who still sports a contacts list on your PC or Mac. If so, you can export that list to your Tab, where your peeps can be added to the horde of friends awaiting in the Contacts app.

The secret to moving your contacts from the computer to the tablet is to save them in the vCard file format. Most email programs, as well as contact management software, provide an option to export contact entries in this file format. (The variety of applications makes it impossible for me to be specific on the steps involved.) Even so, look for a File ⇨ Export command and choose the vCard file format for the contacts you want to share.

After the contacts are saved, transfer the vCard file(s) from the computer to your Tab. Directions are offered in Chapter 18. You want to save the file(s) in the Download folder on the tablet. In the Contacts app, follow these directions to complete the process:

1. **Tap the Action Overflow icon.**

Ensure that it's the Action Overflow by the Search bar, not the one associated with a specific contact.

2. **Choose Manage Contacts.**

3. **Choose Import/Export Contacts.**

4. **Tap the IMPORT button.**

5. **Ensure that the Internal Storage option is chosen.**

The tablet searches for any available vCards. You see the results listed. When no vCard files are located, the process stops. Try again with the file transfer.

6. **Select which vCards you want to import.**

Tap the All option to choose them all.

7. **Tap the DONE button.**

No, you're not done yet.

8. **Choose your Google account.**

You may see other accounts listed, such as Yahoo!. Choose the account to which you want to import the contacts. Do not choose the Tablet option.

9. **Tap the IMPORT button.**

Now you're done.

Also see the later section "Joining identical contacts" in case you merged someone already in the address book.

Manage Your Friends

Nothing is truly perfect the first time, especially when you create things on a Galaxy Tab while typing with your thumbs at 34,000 feet during turbulence. You can do a whole spate of things with (and to) your friends in the tablet's address book. This section covers the more interesting and useful things.

Editing contact information

To make minor touch-ups to any contact, locate and display the contact's information in the Contacts app. Tap the EDIT button.

Change or add information by tapping a field and typing with the onscreen keyboard. You can edit information as well: Tap the field to edit and change whatever you want.

Some information cannot be edited. For example, fields pulled in from a social networking site can be edited only by the account holder on that social networking site.

When you've finished editing, tap the SAVE button.

Taking a picture of a contact

Nothing can be more delicious than snapping an inappropriate picture of someone you know and using the picture as his contact picture on your Tab. Then every time he contacts you, that embarrassing, potentially career-ending photo comes up.

I suppose you could use nice pictures as well, but what's the fun in that?

To use the tablet's camera to snap a contact picture, heed these directions:

1. **Locate and display the contact's information.**

2. **Touch the contact's picture.**

   If no picture is currently assigned, you see a placeholder or often the Camera icon.

   Upon success, you see a card with the Tab's camera on top and preset images appearing below. An icon to link to the Gallery app is also provided.

3. **Use the tablet's camera to snap a picture.**

   Chapter 12 covers using the camera. Both the front and rear cameras can be used (but not both at the same time). Tap the Shutter icon to take the picture.

4. **Review the picture.**

   Nothing is set yet. If you want to try again, tap the Red Minus button, shown in the margin.

5. **Tap the SAVE button to confirm the new image.**

   The image now appears whenever the contact is referenced on your tablet.

To remove an image from a contact, you need to edit the contact as described in the preceding section. Tap the contact's picture while you're editing, and then tap the Red Minus button to remove the image.

You can also use any image stored on the tablet as a contact's picture. In Step 3, choose the Gallery icon. Browse for and select an image, and then crop.

Making a favorite

A *favorite* is a special type of contact, perhaps people you frequently stay in touch with, though not necessarily people you like. Making a contact a favorite places the person in the Favorites group, which is accessed by tapping the Favorites item in the Contacts app index.

 To add a contact to the Favorites group, display the contact's information and tap the Favorite (Star) icon by the contact's image. When the star is gold, the contact is one of your favorites and is listed in the Favorites group.

To remove a favorite, tap the contact's star again, and it loses its color. Removing a favorite doesn't delete the contact.

By the way, a contact has no idea whether he's one of your favorites, so don't believe that you're hurting his feelings by not making him a favorite.

Joining identical contacts

The Galaxy Tab can pull in contacts from multiple sources (Facebook, Gmail, Twitter), so you may find duplicate contact entries. Rather than fuss over which to use, you can join similar contacts. Here's how:

1. **Wildly scroll the Contacts list until you locate a duplicate.**

   Well, maybe not *wildly* scroll, but locate a duplicated entry. Because the address book is sorted, duplicates usually appear close together.

2. **Select one of the duplicate contacts.**

3. **Tap the Action Overflow icon on the contact's card and choose Link Contact.**

   The card that appears lists some contacts that the tablet guesses could be identical. It might be spot-on. Also displayed is the entire Contacts list, in case the tablet guesses incorrectly. Your job is to find the duplicate contact.

4. **Select the duplicate contact from the list.**

5. **Tap the LINK button.**

The accounts are merged, appearing as a single entry in the Contacts app.

Separating contacts

The topic of separating contacts has little to do with parenting, though separating bickering children is the first step to avoid a fight. Contacts in the address book might not be bickering, but occasionally the tablet may automatically join two contacts who aren't really the same person. When that happens, you can split them by following these steps:

1. **Display the contact that comes from two separate sources.**

Sometimes it's difficult to spot such a contact. An easy way for me is when I see two diverse email addresses for the contact or an incorrect picture. Either situation could indicate a mismatch.

2. **Touch the Action Overflow icon on the contact's card and choose Manage Linked Contacts.**

You see a list of contact sources,.

3. **Tap the UNLINK button by the account you want to separate.**

You don't need to actively look for improperly joined contacts as much as you'll just stumble across them. When you do, feel free to separate them, especially if you detect any bickering.

Removing a contact

Every so often, consider reviewing your contacts. Purge those folks whom you no longer recognize or have forgotten. Follow these steps:

1. **View the forlorn contact.**

2. **Tap the Action Overflow and choose Delete.**

3. **Tap the DELETE button to confirm.**

This question is important: Deleting an account from your Tab also deletes it from the account with which it's associated. So, if the contact is a Google contact, it's removed from Google on the Internet as well as from all your Android mobile devices.

Poof! They're gone.

>> For some linked accounts, the Contacts app doesn't let you delete the account. Instead, you need to remove the account from the linked source, such as Facebook.

>> Removing a contact doesn't kill the person in real life.

Chapter **7**

Mail of the Electronic Kind

Tell someone that you don't have an email address and he'll look at you as if you've just told him that you use candles instead of electric lights. Truly, having an email address is a sure sign that you're a citizen of the 21st century.

To help you meet your email and connectivity demands, the Galaxy Tab provides two apps: Email and Gmail. The Gmail app is specific to Google's email, though it can also handle other email accounts. The Email account doesn't do Gmail. Therefore, I cover using only the Gmail app in this chapter.

Galactic Email

You could use the tablet's web browser app to fetch and compose your email epistles. This solution works, but the interface gets clunky. A better solution is to use the Gmail app, which is already associated with your Gmail account, the primary account on your Galaxy Tab. As a bonus, you can add other email accounts, making Gmail the one and only app for your electronic mail duties.

>> Other email apps are available, such as those customized to a specific email service. For example, if you use Yahoo! Mail, consider getting the Yahoo! Mail app from Google Play. It ties in better with your Yahoo! account than the Gmail app.

>> If you forget your Gmail password, visit this web address:

```
google.com/accounts/ForgotPasswd
```

Adding more email accounts

Do you remember setting up the first email account for your Tab? No? You did it when you first configured the device. It was your Gmail account. You probably have more email accounts. Time to add them now:

1. **Open the Gmail app.**

2. **Tap the Side Menu icon to display the navigation drawer.**

3. **Choose Settings.**

   You see the Settings screen, which lists current email accounts associated with the Gmail app.

4. **Choose Add Account.**

   The Set Up Email card appears, listing several categories of email:

   Google: Add another Gmail account.

   Outlook, Hotmail, and Live: Choose this option for various types of Microsoft accounts, though if you have a corporate Exchange Server account, use the Exchange and Office 365 option instead.

   Yahoo!: Add your Yahoo! Mail account.

   Exchange and Office 365: Add your corporate email account hosted by an Exchange Server or Office 365 email account. It's best that you get details on this type of email account from your organization's IT department.

   Other: Choose this option when your email service doesn't match any other category.

5. **Type your email address and tap the NEXT button.**

TIP

Long-press the onscreen keyboard's .com key to see other top-level domains: .net, .org., and so on.

6. **Type the email account password and tap the NEXT button.**

The Gmail app is smart enough at this point to complete configuration, though you may be prompted for further account details. For example, for an Exchange Server account, you may be asked for the domain or other security information.

7. **Set account options.**

These include notifications, synchronization, and download over Wi-Fi. I just leave all the items checked.

It's normal for some Exchange Server accounts to gain remote control over your Tab. You'll see a Device Administrator screen that displays the details. Tap the ACTIVATE button to proceed. You may also need to update the Tab's screen lock to a fully secure setting.

8. **Tap the NEXT button.**

9. **Name the account and set your name for outgoing messages.**

The account name helps you identify the email account. The name is often better than your email address. The app probably guesses correctly on your own name, though you can edit it as well.

10. **Tap the NEXT button.**

The account is set up and appears in the list of accounts on the Gmail app's Settings screen. Tap the Back navigation icon to return to the main Gmail app screen and read your messages.

Repeat these steps to add more accounts.

TIP

If you need to edit an account, follow Steps 1 through 3 in this section, and then tap the account name on the Settings screen.

Creating a signature

I highly recommend that you create a custom email signature for sending messages from your tablet. Here's my signature:

```
DAN
This was sent from my Galaxy Tab.
Typos, no matter how hilarious, are unintentional.
```

To create a signature for an account in the Gmail app, obey these directions:

1. **Tap the Side Menu icon.**

2. **Choose Settings.**

3. **Tap a specific account in the list.**

4. **Choose Mobile Signature.**

   This item may not be available for all types of email accounts.

5. **Use the onscreen keyboard to type a signature.**

   If the account already has a signature, you can delete or edit it.

6. **Tap OK to set the signature.**

Repeat Steps 4 through 6 for each of your Email accounts.

Removing an email account

When you no longer use an email account, purge it from your Tab. Heed these directions while using the Gmail app:

1. **Tap the Side Menu icon and choose Settings from the navigation drawer.**

2. **On the Settings screen, tap the Action Overflow and choose Manage Accounts.**

   The Settings app opens, though the screen that's displayed is accessed only from the Gmail app.

3. **Choose the account you want to banish.**

4. **Tap the REMOVE ACCOUNT button.**

5. **Tap REMOVE ACCOUNT to confirm.**

   The account is no longer associated with your tablet.

Any messages associated with the account are purged from the Gmail app. Exchange Server data, such as contacts and appointments, are also removed.

You've Got Email

You're alerted to the arrival of a new email message in your tablet by a notification icon; the New Gmail notification (shown in the margin) appears at the top of the touchscreen.

Pull down the notifications shade to review pending email. You see either a single notification representing the most recent message or a running total of the number of pending messages. Tap the notification to visit the Gmail app to read the message.

Checking the inbox

To peruse your Gmail, start the Gmail app. Figure 7-1 illustrates the combined inbox, shown as All Mail. This presentation shows messages from all email accounts added to the Gmail app.

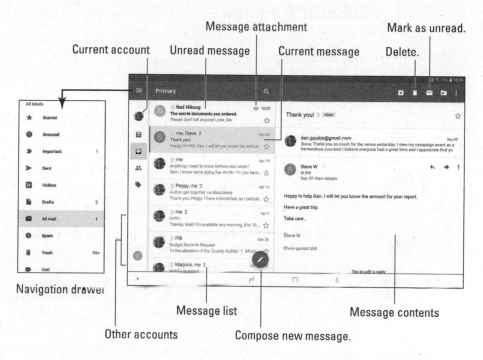

FIGURE 7-1:
The Gmail inbox.

Messages appear in a list, shown in the center in Figure 7-1. Tap a message to view its contents, shown on the right. Tap the Side menu icon to view the navigation drawer, from which you can select message folders and other interesting items.

>> If you rotate the tablet vertically, the inbox view changes: You see only the message list or a message's contents.

>> In the Gmail app, messages are collected in *threads:* You see the original message at the bottom of the thread and then any replies stacked above. Sometimes the messages are hidden; tap the Number icon to view the details.

» To mark a message as unread after you've read it, tap the Unread icon, illustrated in Figure 7-1.

» To view messages associated with a specific account, tap that account bubble listed on the left side of the screen. The current account is shown at the top, other accounts appear at the bottom. Not every account has an image, as shown in Figure 7-1.

» To view all messages, tap the side menu icon and choose All Mail from the navigation drawer.

Reading email

As mail comes in, you can read it by choosing the New Email notification or tapping the message entry in the Gmail app. To work with the message, use the icons that appear above the message. These icons, which may not look exactly like those shown in the margin, cover common email actions:

Reply: Tap this icon to reply to a message. A new message card appears with the To and Subject fields filled in based on the original message.

Reply All: Tap this icon to respond to everyone who received the original message, including folks on the Cc line. This command might be found by tapping the Action Overflow icon.

Forward: Tap this icon to send a copy of the message to someone else.

Delete: Tap this icon to delete the message.

To access additional email commands, touch the Action Overflow icon. For example, to print a message, choose Print from the Action Overflow.

WARNING

» Use Reply All only when everyone else must get a copy of your reply. Because most people find endless Reply All email threads annoying, use the Reply All option judiciously.

» Starred messages in Gmail can be viewed or searched separately, making them easier to locate later.

Write That Message

 To get mail, you must send mail. Composition is done in the Gmail app by tapping the Compose icon, illustrated in Figure 7-1 and shown in the margin. The Gmail composition screen appears, shown in Figure 7-2.

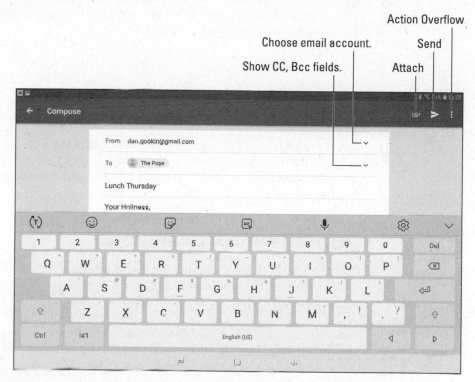

FIGURE 7-2:
Writing a new
Gmail message.

If you have multiple email accounts installed on the Tab, tap the From field to choose another one.

Tap the To field to enter the recipient's address; just type the first few letters and then choose a matching contact name.

Fill in the Subject field. Type the message. Tap the Send icon (labeled in Figure 7-2) to whisk off the message. Or, if you'd rather save the message and work on it later, tap the Action Overflow icon and choose Save Draft.

>> To cancel a message, tap the Action Overflow and choose Discard. If prompted, tap the DISCARD button to confirm.

>> To work on a draft you've saved, tap the Side Menu icon (refer to Figure 7-1) and choose Drafts. Choose a draft message in the list, and then tap the Edit (pencil) icon, shown in the margin, in the message to continue editing.

>> To summon the Cc and Bcc fields, touch the +CC/BCC icon, shown in Figure 7-2.

>> You can also generate a new message from the Contacts app: Locate the contact to whom you want to send the electronic missive. Tap the contact's email address to begin composing a message.

TIP

Message Attachments

The key to understanding attachments in the Gmail app is to look for the Attach icon, similar to what's shown in the margin. After you locate this icon, you can either deal with an attachment for incoming email or add an attachment to outgoing email.

Dealing with attachments

Photo attachments appear directly in an email message, which is logical and convenient. To save the attachment, long-press it and choose View Image. On the next screen, you can tap the Action Overflow to choose what to do with the image.

Non-image attachments may show up as previews or as cards, as shown in Figure 7-3, which lists the attachment's name and two icons. The first icon downloads the attachment; the second icon varies, depending on which app may open the attachment or which app you've used previously to deal with the attachment.

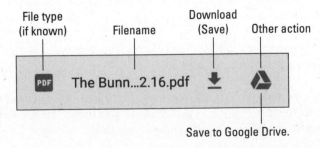

FIGURE 7-3: Attachment methods and madness.

If you don't know what to do with the attachment, tap the card. The appropriate app may open the file, or you may see an Open With card full of apps that can deal with the attachment. If so, tap an icon to open the attachment in that app.

>> When you encounter an attachment that cannot be opened, you must either suffer through not viewing the attachment or reply to the message and direct the person to resend the attachment in a common file format.

>> Common file formats include PNG and JPEG for pictures, and HTML or RTF for documents. PDF, or Adobe Acrobat, documents are also common. Your Galaxy tablet should have no trouble opening them.

>> Look for saved attachments by using the My Files app. Choose the Download item from the left side of the screen to peruse recent downloads. Attachments you save may also generate a Download Complete notification icon; choose that notification to view the attachment.

Sending an attachment

You have two methods for sending an email attachment from the Galaxy Tab. The tablet way is to find the attachment source and use a Share command to stick it in an email message. The traditional, computer way of sending an attachment is to first create the message and then attach the item.

 Most apps that create or view information feature a Share command. Look for the Share icon, similar to what's shown in the margin. View the item you want to share — a picture, a video, music, a text message, or what-have-you — and then touch the Share icon. Choose the Gmail app and then compose a message as described in this chapter. The item you choose to share is automatically attached to the message.

The second way to share is to compose a new message and tap the Attach icon, such as the one shown earlier, in Figure 7-2. Follow the directions on the screen to hunt down the attachment.

>> When you compose a message and then add an attachment, you start by choosing the app that lets you access the attachment and then find the attachment itself. For example, to add a photo, choose the Photos app and then look for the image you want to attach. Unlike when you're using a computer, you don't just hunt down a specific file.

>> It's possible to attach multiple items to a single email message. Just keep tapping the Attachment icon to add goodies.

>> The variety of items you can attach depends on which apps are installed on the tablet.

Chapter **8**

Text, Video, and Voice Chat

The LTE Galaxy Tab has a phone number. It's not a dial-up phone number; your cellular provider merely uses the number to bill you. So, as far as phone calls are concerned, you're as out of luck as owners of the Wi-Fi-only tablets. That's no cause for despair, however, because your Galactic tablet is more than capable of placing — and receiving — phone calls. All you need are the proper apps, which also provide tools for text chat, video chat, and even text messaging.

Let's Hang Out

One way that you can fool your Galaxy Tab into acting more like a phone is to use the Hangouts app. It does text chat, voice, and video chat. It can even place phone calls, when properly equipped. The only downside to the app is that you can communicate only with your friends who have Google accounts.

Using Hangouts

The Hangouts app can be found on the Apps screen. You might also look for it inside the Google folder on the Home screen. And if you still can't find it, you can obtain the app from Google Play. It's free! See Chapter 16.

When you first start the Hangouts app, it may ask whether you want to make phone calls. Of course you do! Install the Hangouts Dialer — Call Phones app. If you're not prompted, get that app from Google Play.

The Hangouts app listens for incoming conversation requests; you can also start your own. You can even do other things on the tablet — you're alerted via notification of an impending Hangouts request; the Hangouts notification icon is shown in the margin.

REMEMBER

>> Conversations are archived in the Hangouts app. To peruse a previous text chat, select it from the list. Video calls aren't archived, but you can review when the call took place and with whom.

>> To remove a previous conversation, long-press it. Tap the Trash icon that appears atop the screen.

>> Your friends can use Hangouts on a computer or a mobile device; it doesn't matter which. But they must have a camera available to enable video chat.

Typing at your friends

The most basic form of communication in the Hangouts app — and one of the oldest forms of communications on the Internet — is text chat, in which people type text back and forth at each other. It can be most tedious. I'll be brief:

1. **Tap the Conversation tab.**

   The Conversation Tab icon is shown in the margin.

2. **Choose a previous conversation to continue, or tap the Add icon to start a new conversation.**

   If you tap the Add icon, choose New Conversation and type the contact's name, email, or phone number into the prompt provided.

3. **Use the onscreen keyboard to type a message, as shown in Figure 8-1.**

4. **Tap the Send icon to send your comment.**

   The Send icon replaces the Attachment icon when you type a message.

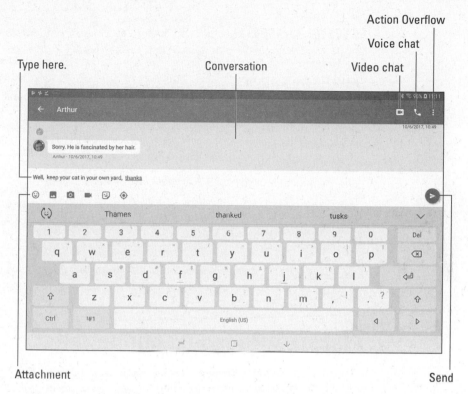

FIGURE 8-1:
Text chatting.

You type, your friend types, and so on until you grow tired or the tablet's battery dies.

TIP

To chat with multiple friends, tap the Action Overflow icon on the chat screen and choose People. Tap the Add People button to type another name, email, or phone number, or pluck various people as listed on the screen.

Talking and video chat

Take the hangout up a notch by tapping the Voice Chat icon, shown in the margin and in Figure 8-1. When you do, your friend receives a pop-up invite. After that person taps the Accept icon, you begin talking.

To see the other person, tap the Video Chat icon, shown in the margin. As soon as they agree, you can see each other. Ensure that you're properly attired before you tap this icon.

To end the call, tap the red End Call button, like ending a phone call on an Android phone. Well, say goodbye first, and then tap the icon.

>> During the chat, the person you're talking with appears in the big window; you're in the smaller window. That's in case you don't remember what you look like.

>> If other people join the conversation, they appear in smaller windows at the bottom of the screen. Tap a window to enlarge it.

>> To mute the call, tap the Microphone icon.

>> Tap the Video icon to disable the camera and return to voice or text chat.

>> The onscreen controls may vanish after a second; tap the screen to see the controls again.

>> Video calls aren't archived, but you can review when the call took place and with whom by choosing a video chat item.

Placing a Hangouts phone call

If you've obtained the Hangouts Dialer app, you can use the Hangouts app to place a real, live phone call. It's amazingly simple, and it works like this:

1. **Tap the Phone Calls tab in the Hangouts app.**

   Refer to Figure 8-1 for its location. If you don't see the Phone Calls tab, you haven't installed the Hangouts Dialer app yet.

2. **Type a contact name or a phone number.**

3. **Tap the matching contact, or tap the phone number (when it doesn't belong to a contact) to dial.**

   The call is placed.

 If you'd rather dial a number directly, tap the Dialpad icon, shown in the margin. Type the phone number, and then tap the green Dial icon to place the call.

Tap the red End Call icon when you're done.

>> To the person you're calling, an incoming Hangouts call looks just like any other call, although the number may be displayed as *Unavailable*.

>> The good news: Calls are free!

>> The bad news: Not every number can be dialed by using the Hangouts app.

Connect to the World with Skype

More popular and ancient than the Hangouts app is Skype. It's the traditional way to place phone calls on the Internet, including inexpensive international calls. Despite the growing popularity of Google Hangouts, Skype remains one of the most popular Internet communications tools.

Getting Skype for your Tab

Your Galaxy Tab most likely didn't come with the Skype app, so visit Google Play and obtain the app. If you find multiple Skype apps, get the one from the Skype company itself.

To use Skype, you need a Skype account. If you already have one, sign in when you first start the app. Otherwise, you can sign up when the app starts.

REMEMBER

>> When you start the Skype app for the first time, work through the start-up screens and take the tour. Be sure to have Skype scour the tablet's address book (the Contacts app) for contacts you can Skype. This process may take a while, but if you're just starting out, it's a great help.

>> Skype is free to use. Text chat is free. Voice and video chat with one other Skype user is also free. But if you want to call a real phone or video chat with a group, you need to boost your account with Skype Credit.

>> You can use video chat with Google Hangouts without having to pay extra.

>> Don't worry about getting a Skype number, which costs extra. It's necessary only if you expect to receive phone calls on your tablet by using Skype.

Chatting with another Skype user

Text chat with Skype works similarly to texting on a smartphone. The only difference is that the other person must be a Skype user. So in that respect, Skype text chat works a lot like Google Hangouts chat, covered elsewhere in this chapter.

To chat, follow these steps:

1. **Start the Skype app and sign in.**

   You don't need to sign in when you've previously run the Skype app. Like all other apps, Skype continues to run until you sign out or turn off the tablet.

2. **At the main Skype screen, choose a person to chat with to continue an existing conversation or tap the Edit (Pencil) icon start a new chat.**

3. **Type some text in the Type a Message text box.**

4. **Tap the blue arrow to send the message.**

   As long as your Skype friend is online and eager, you'll be chatting in no time.

You don't need to formally end your chat session. Switch away to another app or lock the tablet. A Skype notification, shown in the margin, floats in should the other party continue the conversation. You'll also see the Skype notification when someone else initiates a chat with you.

Seeing on Skype (video call)

Placing a video call with Skype on your Galaxy tablet is easy: Begin a text chat as described in the preceding section. After the conversation starts, tap the Video Call icon, as shown in the margin. The call rings through to the contact, and if the person wants to video chat, he picks up in no time and you're talking and looking at each other.

Placing a Skype phone call

Ah. The big enchilada: Skype can be used to turn your Galaxy Tab — be it LTE or Wi-Fi — into a smartphone. It's an amazing feat. And it works quite well, providing you have Skype Credit.

To ensure that you have Skype Credit, tap the Account icon on the main Skype screen. Tap the Add Funds button by the Skype to Phone item. Complete the steps presented to fill your Skype account with a modest amount of moolah.

With Skype Credit established, you can use the tablet to make a "real" phone call, which is a call to any phone number on the planet (Planet Earth). Heed these steps:

Calls

1. **Tap the Calls icon.**

2. **Tap the Dialpad icon.**

   The Dialpad icon is shown in the margin.

3. **Use the keypad to punch in the phone number.**

   The preset +1 (prefix) is required for dialing to the United States, even when the number is local. Don't erase it!

TIP

For international dialing, the number begins with a plus sign (+) followed by the county code and then the phone number.

4. **Tap the phone (Dial) button at the bottom of the screen to place the call.**

5. **Talk.**

   As you talk, the cost of the call is displayed on the screen. That way, you can keep a tab on the toll.

6. **To end the call, tap the End Call button.**

Lamentably, you can't receive a phone call using Skype unless you pay for a Skype online number. In that case, you can use Skype to both send and receive regular phone calls. This book doesn't cover the Online Number option.

TIP

>> I recommend getting a good headset if you plan to use Skype often to place phone calls.

>> In addition to having to pay the per-minute cost, you may be charged a connection fee for making the call.

>> You can check the Skype website (www.skype.com) for a current list of call rates, for both domestic and international calls.

>> Unless you've paid Skype to have a specific phone number, the phone number shown on the recipient's Caller ID screen is something unexpected — often, merely the text *Unknown*. You might therefore want to email the person you're calling and let her know that you're placing a Skype call. That way, the call won't be skipped because the Caller ID isn't recognized.

Chapter **9**

Web Browsing

The World Wide Web was designed to be viewed on a computer. The monitor is big and roomy. Web pages are displayed amply, like Uncle Ron on the sofa watching a ballgame. The smaller the screen, the more difficult it is to view web pages designed for those roomy monitors. Still, the Galaxy Tab has a delight-fully roomy screen. Further, the web has adapted itself to mobile viewing. You won't miss any information, especially after you've read the tips and suggestions in this chapter.

TIP

» If you have an LTE Tab, activate the Wi-Fi connection before you venture out on the web. Though you can use the mobile data connection, the Wi-Fi connection incurs no data usage charges.

» Many places you visit on the web can instead be accessed more effectively by using specific apps. To visit Facebook, Gmail, Twitter, YouTube, and other popular online services, use an app instead of visiting the website. Check Google Play to see whether your favorite website has its own app.

» One thing you cannot do with your Android is view Flash animations, games, or videos on the web. The web browser app disables the Flash plug-in, also known as Shockwave. I know of no method to circumvent this limitation.

The Web Browser App

The Galaxy Tab comes with two web browser apps: Internet and Chrome.

Internet is Samsung's web browser. It's essentially the Chrome app, but all gussied up by Samsung.

Chrome is Google's web browser app, the default web browser app for all Android devices. Because of its consistency, and seamless integration with other Google apps and Chrome on desktop and laptop computers, I cover Chrome exclusively in this chapter.

Mobile Web Browsing

Rare is the person these days who has had no experience with the World Wide Web. More common is someone who has used the web on a computer but has yet to taste the Internet waters on a mobile device. If that's you, consider this section your quick mobile web orientation.

Viewing the web

To browse the web on your Galaxy Tab, open the Chrome app. It's found on the Apps screen, or you might be lucky and locate an app launcher icon on the Home screen.

Figure 9-1 illustrates the Chrome app's interface. The same features appear whenever the tablet is oriented vertically, though when oriented horizontally (as shown in Figure 9-1), web pages look better.

TIP

Here are some handy web-browsing tips for the tablet:

>> Pan the web page by dragging your finger across the touchscreen. You can pan up, down, left, or right when the page is larger than the tablet's screen.

>> Pinch the screen to zoom out, and spread two fingers to zoom in.

>> The page you see may be the *mobile page,* or a customized version of the web page designed for small-screen devices. To see the nonmobile version, tap the Action Overflow icon and choose Desktop Site.

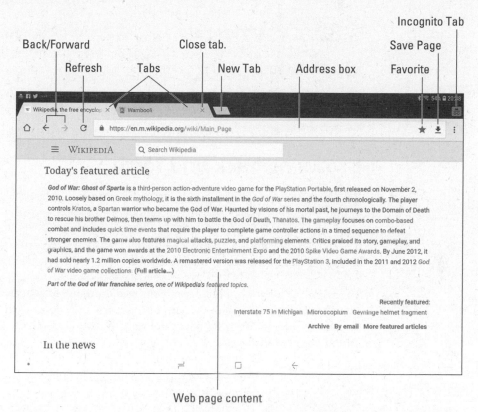

Back/Forward   Refresh   Tabs   Close tab.   New Tab   Address box   Favorite   Save Page   Incognito Tab

FIGURE 9-1:
The Chrome app.

Web page content

Visiting a web page

To visit a web page, type its address into the Address box (labeled in Figure 9–1). You can also type a search word or phrase if you don't know an exact web page address. Tap the Go button on the onscreen keyboard to search the web or to visit a specific web page.

If you don't see the Address box, swipe down the screen.

To "click" links on a page, tap them with your finger. If you have trouble stabbing the correct link, zoom in on the page and try again. Sometimes a tiny magnifier appears when tapping a link. The magnifier helps you poke the right item, though you can't control when and how the magnifier appears.

>> The onscreen keyboard may change some keys to make it easier to type a web page address. Look for a www (World Wide Web) or .com (dot-com) key.

>> Long-press the .com key to see other top-level domains, such as .org and .net.

TIP

>> To reload a web page, touch the Refresh icon on the left end of the Address box. You can also swipe down the page from just under the Tab's status bar to about midscreen. This action, called a *tug,* also refreshes a page.

>> To stop a web page from loading, touch the X that appears to the right of the Address box. The X replaces the Refresh icon.

Browsing back and forth

To return to a web page, you can tap the Chrome app's Back icon (labeled in Figure 9-1) or the Back navigation icon (shown in the margin).

Tap the Chrome app's Forward icon to go forward or to return to a page you were visiting before you touched the Back icon.

To review the long-term history of your web browsing adventures, tap the Action Overflow in the upper right corner of the screen and choose History. The History list shows recently browsed pages not only on your Tab but for Chrome used on other devices as well.

>> See the later section "Clearing your web history" for information on purging items from the History list.

>> Also see the section "Managing web pages in multiple tabs," for information on going incognito instead of constantly purging your browser history.

Working with bookmarks

Bookmarks are those electronic breadcrumbs you can drop as you wander the web. Need to revisit a website? Just look up its bookmark. This advice assumes, of course, that you bothered to create a bookmark when you first visited the site. Bother with these steps in the Chrome app:

1. **Navigate to the web page you must bookmark.**

2. **Tap the Favorite icon.**

The page is bookmarked, but you want to do more with the bookmark. So, quickly:

3. **Tap the EDIT button that appears at the bottom of the screen.**

The Edit Bookmark card appears. All the fields are preset for you, though you may not be entirely pleased with the settings.

4. **If you're an organized person, tap the Folder button to set a specific folder for the bookmark.**

   Mobile bookmarks are set for your Tab only. If the bookmark is one that you want to access on other devices, choose the Bookmarks Bar to save the bookmark.

5. **Type or edit the bookmark's name.**

   I prefer short, punchy names as opposed to long, meandering text.

6. **Tap the Back icon to complete editing the bookmark.**

To see all bookmarks, tap the Action Overflow and choose Bookmarks. To visit a bookmark, tap its entry in the list.

Remove a bookmark by long-pressing its entry in the Bookmarks list. Tap the Delete icon. The bookmark is removed instantly. You can also remove a bookmark by visiting the page again and tapping the Favorite (Star) icon.

TIP

REMEMBER

>> To quickly visit a bookmarked website, just start typing the site's name in the address box. Tap the bookmarked site from the matching list of results displayed below the Address box.

>> Making a favorite web page isn't the same as saving the page. See the later section "Saving a web page."

>> A great way to find which sites to bookmark is to view the web page history: Tap the Action Overflow and choose History.

Managing web pages in multiple tabs

The Chrome app uses a tabbed interface to help you access more than one web page at a time. The tabs march across the screen, as illustrated earlier, in Figure 9-1. Here are the fun things you can do with tabs:

Open a blank tab: To open a blank tab, tap the blank tab stub to the right of the last open tab, illustrated in Figure 9-1.

Open a link in a new tab: To open a link in another tab, long-press the link and choose Open in New Tab.

Open a bookmark in a new tab: To open a bookmark in a new tab, long-press the bookmark and tap the Action Overflow atop the screen. Choose Open in New Tab.

Switch tabs: Tap the tab you want to view.

Close a tab: Tap a tab's Close (X) icon.

You can also switch and close tabs from the Overview: Tap the Recent navigation icon to view the Overview. Tap a tab to switch, or close a tab by swiping its thumbnail off the list.

After you close the last tab, you see a blank screen in the Chrome app. Tap the Add (Plus) icon to summon a new tab.

Going incognito

TIP

Shhh! For private browsing, use an incognito tab: Tap the Action Overflow and choose New Incognito Tab. The incognito tab takes over the screen, changing the look of the Chrome app and offering a description page.

When you go incognito, the web browser doesn't track your history, leave cookies, or provide other evidence of which web pages you've visited. For example, if you go shopping in an incognito window, advertiser tracking cookies won't record your actions. That way, you won't be bombarded with targeted advertising later.

>> When an incognito tab is open, the Incognito notification appears on the phone's status bar, like the one shown in the margin.

>> Choose the incognito notification to close all open incognito tabs.

>> Tap the Incognito icon in the upper right corner of the Chrome app's screen to view any open incognito tabs. (Refer to Figure 9-1.)

REMEMBER

>> The Incognito tab is about privacy, not security. Going incognito doesn't prevent viruses or thwart sophisticated web-snooping software.

Finding text on a web page

To locate text on a web page, tap the Action Overflow and choose Find in Page. Use the onscreen keyboard to type search text. As you type, matching text on the page is highlighted. Use the up and down chevrons to page through found matches.

Tap the Back navigation icon when you've finished searching.

>> The best way to find things on the web is to use the Google widget, found floating on the Home screen.

>> Within the Chrome app, use the Address bar to search the web: Type some search text and tap the onscreen keyboard's Go button.

Sharing a web page

There it is — that web page you just have to talk about to everyone you know! The gauche way to share the page is to copy and paste it. Because you're reading this book, however, you know better. Heed these steps:

1. **Visit the web page you desire to share.**

What's best is to share a link to the page.

2. **Tap the Action Overflow icon and choose Share.**

You see an array of apps and other shortcuts.

3. **Choose an app or a shortcut.**

For example, select Gmail to send the web page's link by email, or select Facebook to share the link with your friends. Social networking apps may list frequent contacts or groups with whom you can share.

4. **Do whatever happens next.**

Whatever happens next depends on how you're sharing the link: Compose the email, write a comment in Facebook, or whatever. Refer to various chapters in this book for specific directions.

You cannot share a page you're viewing on an Incognito tab.

The Art of Downloading

A *download* is a transfer of information over a network from another source to your gizmo. For a Galaxy Tab, that network is the Internet. For this chapter, the other source is a web page.

» The Downloading Complete notification appears after the tablet has downloaded something. Choose that notification to view the download.

» Nope, you don't download programs to your tablet. That's because new apps are obtained from Google Play. See Chapter 16.

» Most people use the term *download* to refer to copying or transferring a file or other information. That's technically inaccurate, but the description passes for social discussion.

TECHNICAL STUFF

» The opposite of downloading is *uploading*. That's the process of sending information from your gizmo to another location on a network.

Grabbing an image from a web page

Downloading an image from a web page is cinchy: Long-press the image. You see a pop-up menu, from which you choose the Download Image action. Tap the DOWNLOAD button to confirm.

To view images you download from the web, you use the Photos app. Downloaded images are saved in the Download album, a device folder: In the Photos app, tap the Side Menu icon and choose Device Folders to access the Download album.

Downloading a file

Your Galaxy Tab tries its best to view some types of links, such as PDF files. When you'd rather save the linked information, long-press the link and choose the Save Link action. The linked file is downloaded to your tablet.

If the Save Link command doesn't appear, the file cannot be downloaded, either because the file is an unrecognized type or because there's a potential security issue.

Saving a web page

To save the entire web page you're viewing, tap the Download icon, shown in the margin. This icon is located on the right end of the address bar.

TECHNICAL STUFF

>> One reason for downloading an entire page is to read it later, especially when the Internet isn't available. This tip is one of my Android travel suggestions. More travel tips are found in Chapter 22.

>> Some web pages load dynamic information. If you open a saved web page and find some of the artwork absent or other features disabled, it's the missing dynamic information that's making the page look odd.

Reviewing your downloads

To access any image, file, or web page you've downloaded or saved on your Tab, follow these steps in the Chrome web browser app:

1. **Tap the Action Overflow.**

2. **Choose Downloads.**

   A list of cards appears on the Downloads screen, each one representing something you've downloaded.

3. **Tap a card to open and view the item you downloaded.**

REMEMBER

You can choose the Download notification to quickly review any single downloaded item.

Web Browser Controls and Settings

More options and settings and controls exist for the Chrome app than just about any other app I've used on a Galaxy Tab. It's complex. Rather than bore you with every dangdoodle detail, I thought I'd present just a few of the options worthy of your attention.

Clearing your web history

When you don't want the entire Internet to know what you're looking at on the web, open an Incognito tab, as described earlier in the section "Going incognito." When you forget to do that, follow these steps to clear one or more web pages from the browser history:

1. Tap the Action Overflow and choose History.

2. Tap the X icon next to the web page entry you want to remove.

   The evidence is erased.

If you want to remove *all* of your web browsing history, after Step 1 tap the CLEAR BROWSING DATA button. You see the Clear Browsing Data screen. The preselected items are the ones you need, so tap the CLEAR DATA button to rid your Android of your sordid past.

Changing the way the web looks

No matter which size of Galactic tablet you own, you have several ways to improve the way the web looks. First and foremost, don't forget that you can orient the device horizontally or vertically, which rearranges the way a web page is displayed.

From the Settings screen, you can also adjust the zoom setting used to display a web page. Heed these steps when using the Chrome app:

1. Tap the Action Overflow icon and choose Settings.

2. Choose Accessibility.

3. Use the Text Scaling slider to adjust the text scaling.

You can spread your fingers to zoom in on any web page.

Setting privacy and security options

As far as the Chrome app's security settings go, most of the options are already enabled. If information retained on the tablet concerns you, you can clear it. Obey these steps:

1. **Tap the Action Overflow icon and choose Settings.**

2. **Choose Autofill and Payments.**

3. **Choose Address and More.**

4. **Slide the master control to the Off position.**

5. **Tap the Back navigation icon.**

   You return to the main Autofill and Payments screen.

6. **Choose Payment Methods.**

7. **Slide the master control to the Off position.**

8. **Tap the Back navigation icon twice.**

   You're back at the main Settings screen.

9. **Choose Passwords.**

10. **Slide the master control to the Off position.**

With regard to general online security, my advice is always to be smart and think before doing anything questionable on the web. Use common sense. One of the most effective ways that the Bad Guys win is by using *human engineering* to try to trick you into doing something you normally wouldn't do, such as click a link to see a cute animation or a racy picture of a celebrity or politician. As long as you use your noggin, you should be safe.

Also see Chapter 21 for information on applying a secure screen lock to your Tab.

IN THIS CHAPTER

» **Getting Facebook**

» **Sharing your life on Facebook**

» **Sending pictures to Facebook**

» **Tweeting on Twitter**

» **Exploring other social networking opportunities**

Chapter **10**

Social Networking

The Internet is amazing. It has greatly expanded mankind's access to knowledge while proving to be the largest time killer in history. Marching forward in support of the second hypothesis, I present you with the topic of social networking.

Armed with your Galaxy tablet, you can keep your digital social life up-to-date wherever you go. You can communicate with your friends, followers, and buddies; upload pictures and videos you take on the tablet; or simply share your personal, private, intimate thoughts with the mass of humanity.

Face-to-Face with Facebook

Of all the social networking sites, Facebook is the king. It's the online place to go to catch up with friends, send messages, express your thoughts, share pictures and videos, play games, and waste more time than you ever thought you had.

» Though you can access Facebook on the web by using the tablet's web browser app, I highly recommend that you use the Facebook app, described in this section.

» If your Tab doesn't have the Facebook app preinstalled, obtain it from Google Play. See Chapter 16.

» You can use the Facebook app to sign up for a Facebook account, or you can sign in with your existing account.

» After signing in to Facebook the first time, you must perform configuration. I recommend choosing the option to synchronize Facebook with your Android's Contacts app. You must grant permission for the app to access your contacts; tap the ALLOW button when prompted.

TIP

Running Facebook on your tablet

The main Facebook screen has several tabs, shown in Figure 10-1. The primary tab is the News Feed. Options for interacting with Facebook appear at the bottom of the screen.

FIGURE 10-1:
Facebook on a Galaxy Tab.

To set Facebook aside, tap the Home navigation icon to return to the Home screen. The Facebook app continues to run until you either sign out of the app or turn off your device.

To sign out of the Facebook app, tap the More icon (refer to Figure 10-1) and choose the Log Out action (from the bottom of the list). Tap the LOG OUT button to confirm.

>> To update the News Feed, tug downward on the screen: Swipe from just below the status bar to the center of the touchscreen.

>> Use the Like, Comment, or Share icons below a News Feed item to like, comment, or share something, respectively. Existing comments appear only when you choose the Comment item.

>> The Facebook app generates notifications for news items, mentions, chats, and so on. This notification icon looks similar to the one shown in the margin.

>> To send instant messages on Facebook, you must obtain a separate app. The Facebook app bugs you to install the Messenger app, prompting eternally until you do so.

Setting your status

The primary thing you live for on Facebook, besides having more friends than anyone else, is to update your status. It's the best way to share your thoughts with the universe and is far cheaper than skywriting and far less offensive than a robocall.

To set your status, follow these steps in the Facebook app:

1. Switch to the News Feed.

Tap the News Feed icon, labeled in Figure 10-1.

2. Tap the status update area.

This area is highlighted in Figure 10-1. It typically shows the text *What's on your mind?*

Upon success, you see the Create Post screen, where you can type your musings as well as perform other activities, as illustrated in Figure 10-2.

3. Set the post's visibility.

The two main options are Public and Friends, where Public makes the post visible to anyone on Facebook and Friends limits viewing to only your friends.

4. Tap the What's On Your Mind field to type something pithy, newsworthy, or typical of the stuff you read on Facebook.

When you can't think of anything to post, take off your shoes, sit down, and take a picture of your feet against something else in the background. That seems to be really popular.

5. Tap the POST button to share your thoughts.

Choose a sharing audience.

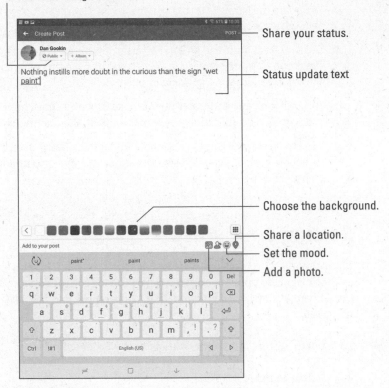

Share your status.

Status update text

Choose the background.

Share a location.

Set the mood.

Add a photo.

FIGURE 10-2:
Updating your
Facebook status.

To cancel the post, tap the Back navigation icon. Tap the Discard Post button to confirm.

TIP

>> If you've added the Facebook widget to the Home screen, you can use that widget to share a quick post.

>> The color palette below the post text lets you set a background color for the post.

>> Other options include adding a photo, setting a location, and so on. When you tap one of these icons (illustrated in Figure 10-2), you see a complete list of potential actions and activities.

Uploading a picture to Facebook

One of the many things your Galaxy Tab can do is take pictures. Combine that feature with the Facebook app and you have an all-in-one gizmo designed for sharing the various intimate and private moments of your life with the ogling throngs of the Internet.

To share a picture or video in the Facebook app, follow these steps:

1. **Update your status.**

   Refer to the preceding section, though you don't need to type any text if you just want to post a photo or video.

2. **Tap the Add Photo icon.**

   Refer to Figure 10-2. After you tap the icon, you see a long slate of potential actions.

3. **Select an image stored on your phone or tablet.**

   You can, optionally, tap additional images to share an album.

4. **Tap the DONE button.**

   The images or videos are presented in the post.

5. **Tap the POST button to share.**

You can also snap a picture or record a video on the spot: In Step 4, tap the Add Photo or Add Video icon, both of which are shown in the margin. Use the device's camera to shoot the image or record a video snippet. Specifics on using the Camera app are covered in Chapter 12.

>> I find it easier to use the Camera app to take a bunch of images or record video and then choose that item later to upload it to Facebook.

>> If you're unhappy with the photo you took, tap the Retry button to take another image, or tap Done / OK and get ready to post the image or video to Facebook. Tap Cancel (in the upper left corner of the screen) to abandon your efforts.

>> Another popular photo-sharing option is 360 Photo, which lets you capture a wider panoramic shot or the entire area around you. Not every device shows this option in the Facebook app.

>> The Facebook app appears on the various Share menus available in other apps on the tablet. Tap the Share icon to send to Facebook a YouTube video, an image, a web page, some music, and so on.

Going live

When you opt to share a video on Facebook, you have several options. You can

>> Share a video that was already recorded and saved.

>> Record a video and then share it.

>> Go live, and share the video as you record it.

The first two options are covered in the preceding section. To go live, choose the Go Live option instead of Photo/Video: Before typing text, look for the Go Live entry in the long list of actions you can perform or add to a Facebook post.

Going live involves using the Tab's camera. You can switch front and rear cameras before or during the recording. Tap the Record icon to start; tap the Stop icon to end the broadcast. See Chapter 12 for more details on using the Tab's Camera app.

The video is presented live to anyone who's on Facebook at the time. You can, optionally, save the video for playback later: Read the prompts after you stop recording.

All A-Twitter

Twitter is a social networking site, similar to Facebook but far briefer. On Twitter, you write short spurts of text that express your thoughts or observations, or you share links. Or, you can use Twitter just to follow the thoughts and twitterings, or *tweets,* of other people.

If your Android didn't come with the Twitter app, obtain it from Google Play, as described in Chapter 16. Install and run the app to sign in to Twitter using an existing account, or create a new account on the spot.

Figure 10-3 illustrates the Twitter app's main screen, which shows the current tweet feed. The Twitter app is updated frequently, so its exact appearance may change after this book has gone to press.

To read tweets, choose the Home category, shown in Figure 10-3. Recent tweets are displayed in a list, with the most recent information at the top. Tug the list downward to update the tweets; swipe from just below the status bar to center screen.

To tweet, tap the New Tweet icon, shown in Figure 10-3. The "What's happening?" screen appears, where you can compose a tweet.

REMEMBER

A tweet has a limited number of characters. An indicator on the New Tweet screen informs you of how many characters remain.

Tap the Tweet button to share your thoughts with the twitterverse.

>> A message posted on Twitter is a *tweet.*

>> You can post messages on Twitter and follow others who post messages. Twitter is a good way to get updates and information quickly, from not only individuals but also news outlets and other organizations.

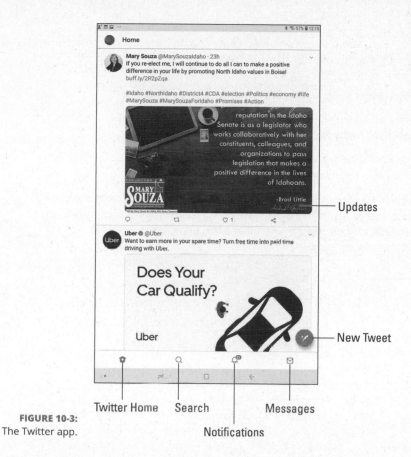

Updates

New Tweet

Twitter Home   Search   Messages

Notifications

FIGURE 10-3:
The Twitter app.

Even More Social Networking

The Internet is nuts over social networking. Facebook may be the king, but lots of landed gentry are out for that crown. It almost seems as though a new social networking site pops up every week. Beyond Facebook and Twitter, other social networking sites include, but are not limited to

>> Google+

>> LinkedIn

>> Meebo

>> MeWe

>> Myspace

Apps for these services are obtained from Google Play. You can use the app itself to sign up for an account or log in by using an existing account.

TIP

>> See Chapter 16 for more information on Google Play.

>> Google+ is Google's social networking app, which is related to the Hangouts app. See Chapter 8 for information on using Hangouts.

>> The HootSuite app can be used to share your thoughts on a multitude of social networking platforms.

>> As with Facebook and Twitter, you may find your social networking apps appearing on Share menus in various apps. That way, you can easily share your pictures and other types of media with your online social networking pals.

3
Everything in the Galaxy

Understand how to find things on the map.

Work with the camera.

View and edit pictures.

Enjoy digital music.

Explore amazing tablet feats.

Shop at Google Play.

Chapter **11**

From Here to There

Stupid kidnappers. They took my phone but left the Galaxy Tab. I suppose they thought it might be a picture frame. Or perhaps they didn't even look inside the fine, imitation leatherette cover, figuring it was a portfolio. That was a mistake.

Even from inside the uncomfortable trunk, I could use the tablet. The screen was bright; the cellular signal was clear. The Maps app told me that I was somewhere in Seattle.

Seattle! Had they driven that far? It wasn't important: Using the tablet, I knew not only where I was but also where a fancy Hungarian restaurant could be found nearby. I could send an email with my location to the authorities and then be chowing down on a hot bowl of goulash in no time. Thank heavens for the Maps app!

There's a Map for That

To find your location, as well as the location of things near and far, summon the Maps app. Good news: You run no risk of improperly folding the Maps app. Better news: The Maps app charts the entire country, including freeways, highways, roads, streets, avenues, drives, bike paths, addresses, businesses, and points of interest.

Using the Maps app

To start the Maps app, choose it from the Apps screen. An App Launcher icon for the Maps app might also be found on the Home screen, in the Google folder.

If you're starting the app for the first time or it has been recently updated, you must agree to the terms and conditions. Do so.

The tablet communicates with global positioning system (GPS) satellites to hone in on your current location. The position is accurate to within a given range, referenced by a blue circle around your location on the map, which also shows which direction the tablet is pointing, as shown in Figure 11-1. If the circle doesn't appear, either your location is pretty darn accurate or you need to zoom in.

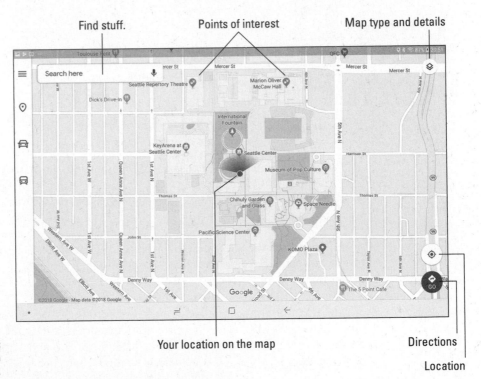

FIGURE 11-1: Your location on a map.

Here are some fun things you can do when viewing the map:

Zoom in: To make the map larger (to move it closer), spread your fingers on the touchscreen.

Zoom out: To make the map smaller (to see more), pinch your fingers on the touchscreen.

Pan and scroll: To see what's to the left or right or at the top or bottom of the map, drag your finger on the touchscreen; the map scrolls in the direction that you drag your finger.

 Rotate: Using two fingers, rotate the map clockwise or counterclockwise. Tap the Compass Pointer icon (shown in the margin) to reorient the map with north at the top of the screen.

Perspective: Touch the screen with two fingers and swipe up or down to view the map in perspective. You can also tap the Location button to switch to Perspective view, though this trick works only for your current location. To return to Flat Map view, tap the Compass Pointer icon.

The closer you zoom in to the map, the more detail you see, such as street names, address block numbers, businesses, and other sites — but no tiny people.

Adding layers

You add details to the map by applying layers: A *layer* can enhance the map's visual appearance, provide more information, or add other fun features to the basic street map, such as Satellite view, shown in Figure 11-2.

 The key to accessing layers is to tap the Map Type and Details icon, shown in the margin. You see the Map Type and Details card, illustrated in Figure 11-2. In the figure, the Satellite layer is chosen. Another popular layer is Traffic, which lists current travel conditions.

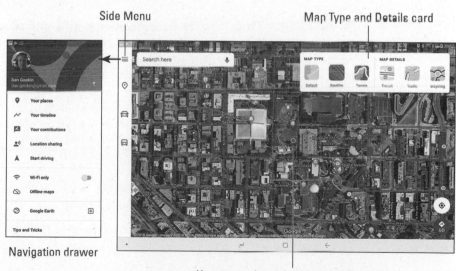

FIGURE 11-2: The Satellite layer.

Side Menu

Map Type and Details card

Navigation drawer

Your approximate location and direction

You don't remove a layer as much as you change back to the Default map type. To return to that view, choose Default from the Map Type and Details card. (Refer to Figure 11-2.)

Saving an offline map

For times when an Internet connection isn't available (which is frequent for a Wi-Fi–only tablet), you can still use the Maps app, though only in a limited capacity. The secret is to save a portion of the map you need to reference. Obey these steps:

1. **View the map chunk you yearn to save.**

   Zoom. Pan. Square in the area to save on the screen. It can be as large or as small as you need. Obviously, smaller maps occupy less storage.

2. **Tap the Side Menu icon.**

3. **Choose Offline Maps from the navigation drawer.**

   Any maps you've previously saved appear in the list.

4. **Tap the SELECT YOUR OWN MAP button.**

   Because you've already selected the map in Step 1, you can move on with Step 5:

5. **Tap the DOWNLOAD button.**

   The map's details are downloaded. Eventually, it appears in the list of offline maps.

To use an offline map, display the navigation drawer and choose Offline Maps. Tap the offline map to view and it shows up on the screen, even when an Internet connection is unavailable. You can browse the map while the device is offline, but you cannot search or use navigation features.

>> Offline maps remain valid for 30 days. After that time, you must update the map to keep it current. A notification reminds you to update.

>> To update an offline map, choose it from the Offline Maps screen and tap the UPDATE button.

>> To name a map something better than MAP1, tap the Action Overflow by the map's entry and choose Rename. Be descriptive.

>> To remove an offline map, choose it and tap the DELETE button. Tap YES to confirm.

It Knows Where You Are

You can look at a physical map all day long, and unless you have a sextant or a GPS, how would you know where you are? Never fear! Your Tab knows where you are. Not only does it have a GPS, but by using the Maps app, it can instantly discover where you are, find what's nearby, and even send your location to someone else.

Finding a location

The Maps app shows your location as a blue dot on the screen. But *where* is that? I mean, if you need to phone a tow truck, you can't just say, "I'm the blue dot on the orange slab by the green thing."

Well, you *can* say that, but it probably won't do any good.

To find your current street address, or any street address, long-press a location on the Maps screen. A card appears at the bottom of the screen that gives your approximate location, plus any items of interest nearby. Tap the card to view more details, as shown in Figure 11-3.

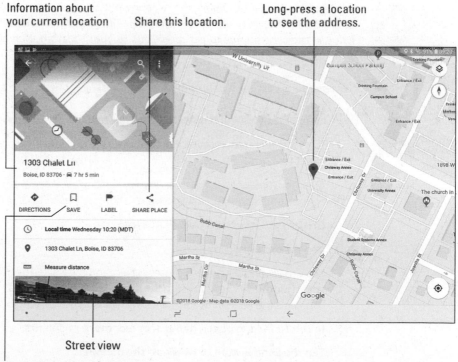

FIGURE 11-3: More info about a location.

Information about your current location

Share this location.

Long-press a location to see the address.

Street view

Mark the location as a favorite.

If you long-press a location, the card features additional information, including perhaps a web page address and contact info.

When you've finished viewing the card, tap the Back navigation icon to return to the main Maps app screen.

» This location trick works only when the tablet has Internet access. When Internet access isn't available, the Maps app is unable to communicate with the Google map servers.

» Use the DIRETIONS button to get directions to the location. See the later section "The Galactic Navigator."

» When you have *way* too much time on your hands, play with the Street View command. Choosing this option displays the location from a 360-degree perspective. In Street view, you can browse a locale, pan and tilt, or zoom in on details — whether you're familiarizing yourself with a location or planning a burglary.

Helping others find your location

It's possible to use the Maps app to send your current location to a friend. If your pal has a mobile device (phone or tablet) with smarts similar to a Galaxy Tab, he can use the coordinates to get directions to your location. Maybe he'll even bring some goulash!

To send your current location in an email message, obey these steps:

1. Long-press your current location on the map.

To see your current location, tap the Location icon in the lower right corner of the Maps app screen.

After long-pressing your location (or any location), you see a card showing the approximate address, similar to what's shown in Figure 11-3.

2. On the card, tap the SHARE PLACE icon.

3. Choose the Gmail app.

The Gmail app starts, with a preset subject and message. The subject is your street address or the address of the card you touched in Step 2. The message content is the address again, but it's also a link to the current location.

4. In the To field, type the name of one or more recipients.

5. Tap the Send button to whisk off the message.

When the recipient receives the email, he can touch the link to open your location in his Android mobile device's Maps app. When the location appears, he can follow my advice in the later section "Getting directions" for finding you. And don't loan him this book; have him buy his own copy. And bring goulash. Thanks.

Find Things

The Maps app can help you find places in the real world, just like the Google app helps you find places on the Internet. Both operations work basically the same: Open the Maps app and, in the Search text box, type something to find. (Refer to Figure 11-1.) You can type a variety of terms in the Search box, as explained in this section.

Looking for a specific address

To locate an address, type it in the Search box; for example:

```
1600 Pennsylvania Ave., Washington, D.C. 20006
```

Tap the Search button on the keyboard, and the location is shown on the map. The next step is getting directions, which you can read about in the later section "Getting directions."

>> You need not type the entire address. Oftentimes, all you need is the street number and street name and then either the city name or zip code.

>> As you're typing, suggestions appear below the Search box. When you see one that matches what you're looking for, tap it.

>> If you omit the city name or zip code, the tablet looks for the closest matching address near your current location.

 >> Tap the X icon in the Search box to clear the previous search.

Finding a business, restaurant, or point of interest

You may not know an address, but you know when you crave sushi or Hungarian or perhaps the exotic flavors of Wyoming. Maybe you need a hotel or a gas station or you must find a place that buys old dentures. To find a business entity or a point of interest, type its name in the Search box; for example:

```
Movie theater
```

This command flags movie theaters on the current Maps screen or nearby.

 To find locations near you, have the Maps app jump to your current location, as described earlier in this chapter. Otherwise, the Maps app looks for places near the area you see on the screen.

Or, you can be specific and look for businesses near a certain location. Specify the city name, district, or zip code, such as:

```
Hungarian Restaurant Seattle
```

After typing this command and touching the Search button, you see whatever Hungarian restaurants are found near Seattle, similar to the one shown on the left in Figure 11-4.

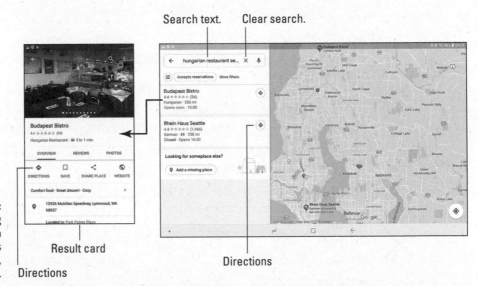

Search text.   Clear search.

FIGURE 11-4:
Finding Hungarian restaurants near Seattle, Washington.

Result card

Directions

Directions

To see more information about a result, tap its card, such as the one for Budapest Bistro in Figure 11-4. When more than one location is found, peruse the list of results (cards) to see more options. After touching a card, you can view more details, similar to what's shown on the left in Figure 11-4.

Tap the DIRECTIONS icon on the restaurant's (or any location's) details screen to get directions; see the later section "Getting directions."

>> Spread your fingers on the touchscreen to zoom in on the map.

>> Every pin or dot on the screen represents a search result. These items match the cards shown.

TIP

>> If you *really* like the location, tap the SAVE icon. That location is kept as one of your favorite places. The location appears as a star on the Maps app screen

Searching for favorite or recent places

Just as you can bookmark favorite websites on the Internet, you can mark favorite places in the real world by using the Maps app. The feature is called Saved Places.

To visit your favorite places or browse your recent map searches, tap the Side Menu icon and choose Your Places from the navigation drawer. Tap the SAVED heading. To revisit a place, tap its entry in the list.

The Galactic Navigator

Finding something is only half the job. The other half is getting there. Your Galaxy Tab is ever ready, thanks to the various direction and navigation features nestled in the Maps app.

WARNING

>> I don't believe that the Galaxy tablet has a car mount — at least the larger models don't. It's not a smartphone, after all. Therefore, I strongly recommend that if you use your Tab in your auto, have someone else hold it and read the directions. Or, use voice navigation, and — for goodness' sake — don't look at the tablet while you're driving!

>> Navigation can consume copious amounts of power. For extra measure, plug the Tab into your car's power supply by using a micro USB car adapter. Such an adapter can be found at electronics stores and similar locations, which you can locate by using the Maps app.

Getting directions

One command associated with locations on the map is getting directions. In the Maps app, the command is coincidentally called DIRECTIONS. Here's how to use it:

1. **Touch the Directions icon in a location's card.**

   Sometimes, you see only the icon, shown in the margin. After touching this icon, you see a screen similar to what's shown in Figure 11-5.

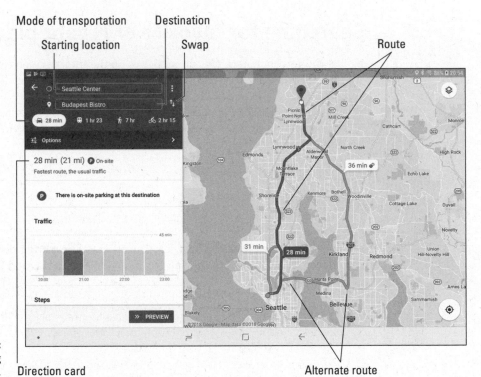

FIGURE 11-5: Planning your trip.

2. **Choose a method of transportation.**

   The available options vary, depending on your location. In Figure 11-5, the items are (from left to right) driving, transit, walking, cycling. An option to use shared transportation, such as Lyft and Uber, may also appear.

3. **Set a starting location.**

   You can type a location or select one of the locations shown on the screen, such as your current location, your home location, or any location you've previously searched. Tap the Starting Location item to choose another location.

4. **Ensure that the starting location and destination are what you want.**

   To reverse them, touch the Swap icon (labeled in Figure 11-5).

5. **Peruse the results.**

The map shows the route, highlighted as a blue line on the screen, as shown in Figure 11-5. Traffic jams and constructions that may delay travel also appear.

To see a list of directions, tap a Direction card. (Refer to Figure 11-5.) A scrolling list appears on the screen, detailing turn-by-turn directions.

> >> If you don't like the route, you can adjust it: Use your finger to drag the blue line. Time and distance measurements shown on the cards change as you adjust the route.

> >> The Maps app alerts you to any toll roads on the specified route. As you travel, you can choose alternative, non-toll routes, if available. You're prompted to switch routes during navigation.

Adding a navigation Home screen widget

When you visit certain places often — such as the liquor store or your parole office — you can save yourself the time you would spend repeatedly typing navigation information. All you need to do is create a navigation widget on the Home screen. Here's how:

1. **Long-press the Home screen and then tap the Widgets icon.**

2. **Choose the Maps widget item.**

3. **Long-press the Directions widget and drag it to a spot on the Home screen.**

   See Chapter 19 for specifics on adding widgets to the Home screen.

4. **Choose a traveling method.**

Your options are by driving, transit, walking, cycling.

5. **In the Choose Destination text box, type a destination, a contact name, an address, or a business.**

6. **Type a shortcut name.**

The name appears below the icon on the Home screen.

7. **Tap the SAVE button.**

The widget is affixed to the Home screen.

Tap the widget to use it. Instantly, the Maps app starts and enters Navigation mode, steering you from wherever you are to the location referenced in Step 5.

Chapter **12**

It's a Big, Flat Camera

Cameras have come a long way since Nicéphore Niépce took a daylong exposure of his backyard using a *camera obscura*. Photography improved over time, but remained an analog, real-world thing until the 1990s. Then technology went digital. In a few more years, no one will be around who remembers what a roll of film was.

What's also changed is the camera. No longer do you hold the thing up to your face. Instead, you hold the device at arm's length and peer at an LCD screen. What's even stranger is holding up a large, flat object such as the Galaxy Tab and using it to take a picture. Sure, it works. It's handy. But it's just unusual and different enough that I present to you an entire chapter on using the tablet as a camera.

Your Galactic Camera

I admit that a Samsung Galaxy Tab isn't the world's best camera. And I'm sure that Mr. Spock's tricorder wasn't the best camera in the *Star Trek* universe, either. That comparison is kind of the whole point: The tablet is an incredible gizmo that does many things. Two of those things are taking pictures and recording video, as described in this section.

Introducing the Camera app

Both picture-taking and video-recording duties on the Galaxy Tab are handled by the same app, the Camera app. You may be able to find a shortcut to this app on the Home screen, and it also dwells with all its app buddies on the Apps screen.

The Camera app controls both the main camera, which is on the tablet's backside, and the front-facing camera, which is not on the tablet's backside.

After starting the Camera app, you see the main Camera screen, as illustrated in Figure 12-1. The tablet's touchscreen serves as the viewfinder; what you see on the screen is exactly what appears in the final photo or video.

— Switch camera.

— Previous Image

— Shutter

— Flash

— Record video.

— Settings

FIGURE 12-1:
The Galaxy Tab
Camera app.

Special shooting modes

>> The tablet can be used as a camera in either landscape or portrait orientation. But:

>> Seriously, take all your pictures and record your videos with the tablet in its horizontal orientation. Beings throughout the galaxy will thank you.

>> The main (rear) camera focuses automatically. To override the automatic focus, tap the screen to move the focus ring and bring a certain part of the image into focus.

>> Zoom in by spreading your fingers on the screen.

>> Zoom out by pinching your fingers on the screen.

TIP

>> You can take as many pictures or record as much video with your tablet as you like, as long as you don't run out of space in the tablet's internal storage or microSD card storage.

>> If your pictures or videos appear blurry, ensure that the camera lens on the back of the tablet isn't dirty. Or perhaps you neglected to remove the plastic cover from the rear camera when you first set up your Tab.

>> See Chapter 13 for information on previewing and managing pictures and videos.

Taking a still image

To take a still picture, tap the Shutter icon. (Refer to Figure 12-1.) The camera focuses, you may hear a mechanical shutter sound, and the flash may go off. You're ready to take the next picture.

To preview the image, touch the Previous Image thumbnail (labeled in Figure 12-1). After viewing the preview, tap the Back navigation icon to return to the Camera app.

TECHNICAL STUFF

>> You can also press the Volume key to snap a photo.

>> Set the image's resolution before you shoot. See the later section "Changing still resolution and video quality."

>> The Galaxy Tab stores pictures in the JPEG image file format, using the .jpg filename extension. The images are stored in the DCIM/Camera folder on either internal storage or the microSD card.

Recording video

To record video on the Galaxy Tab S, tap the Video icon, shown earlier, in Figure 12-1. The icon changes to the Pause icon, and the Shutter icon changes to a Stop icon.

While you're recording, a flashing red dot appears on the screen. You also see a time index and storage information.

Tap the Pause icon to temporarily pause the video. Tap the Record (red dot) icon again to continue the same recording.

Tap the Stop icon when you've finished recording.

Preview the video by tapping the Previous Image icon on the Camera app's screen.

REMEMBER

>> Look for that blinking red dot and time index! You want to ensure that video is recording that you didn't just accidentally take a still shot.

>> Hold the tablet steady when recording video! The camera still works when you whip the tablet around, but wild gyrations render the video unwatchable.

>> Set the video quality before recording video. See the section "Changing still resolution and video quality," later in this chapter.

>> While recording, you can press the Volume key to capture a still image.

TECHNICAL STUFF

>> Videos are stored in the MPEG4 file format, using the .mp4 filename extension. You'll find the videos in the DCIM/Camera folder, either in internal storage or on the microSD card.

Doing a selfie

Who needs to pay all that money for a mirror when you have a Galaxy Tab? You can forget the mirror. Instead, think about taking all those selfies without having to second-guess whether the camera is pointed at your face.

To take your own mug shot, follow these steps:

1. **Start the Camera app.**

2. **Tap the Switch Camera icon.**

When you see yourself on the screen, you're doing it properly.

3. **Snap a still image or record a video.**

Refer to directions earlier in this chapter for details.

Tap the Switch Camera icon again to direct the Tab to again use the main (rear) camera.

Taking in a panorama

No, a *panorama* isn't an exotic new alcoholic drink; it's a wide shot, like a landscape, a beautiful vista, or a family photograph after a garlic feast. To take a panoramic shot using your Galaxy Tab, switch the camera to Panorama mode. Obey these steps:

1. **Start the Camera app.**

2. **Swipe the list of shooting modes to locate and tap the Panorama item.**

   Refer to Figure 12-1 for the location of the shooting modes.

   Directions for capturing a panorama may appear on the screen. Tap the OK button to dismiss.

3. **Hold your arms steady.**

4. **Tap the Shutter icon.**

   You see a frame and a guide on the screen, which approximates the current shot and the extent (left-right or up-down) of the panorama. Arrows point in the directions in which you can pan.

5. **Pivot slightly to your right (or in another direction, but you must continue in the same direction).**

   As you move the camera, the onscreen frame adjusts to your new position. Watch the progress bar on the screen to help keep the panorama even. All you need to do is keep moving.

6. **Tap the Shutter icon again to finish the panorama.**

   After the last image is snapped, wait while the panorama is assembled.

The Camera app sticks the different shots together, creating a panoramic image.

TIP

» It's important that you exit Panorama mode when you're finished. To return the Camera app to normal still-shooting image mode, choose Auto from the list of shooting modes.

» Other shooting modes are available beyond Panorama. For example, Stickers mode lets you add humorous graphics to faces; Pro provides more controls for professional photographers (who probably prefer real cameras over the Galaxy Tab); and HDR activates the High Dynamic Range feature, which enhances the light and dark portions of a still image.

Deleting something you just shot

Disappointed with that image or video? Perhaps someone you love is hanging over your shoulder weeping and begging you to remove it. Hastily follow these steps:

1. **Tap the Previous Image thumbnail that appears on the Camera app's screen. (Refer to Figure 12-1.)**

   After touching the preview, you see the full-screen image. Videos appear with the Play icon center-screen.

2. **Tap the Delete (trash can) icon.**

If you don't see the trash can icon, tap the screen and it shows up.

3. **Tap the DELETE button to confirm.**

4. **Tap the Back navigation icon to return to the Camera app.**

When you desire destruction of more than just the last image you took (or video you recorded), visit the Gallery app. See Chapter 13.

Capturing the screen

A *screen shot,* also called a *screen cap* (for *cap*ture), is a picture of the tablet's touchscreen. So, if you see something interesting on the screen, or just want to take a quick pic of your tablet life, you take a screen shot.

To capture the screen, hold your hand perpendicular to the tablet, like you're giving it a karate chop. Swipe the edge of your palm over the screen, right to left or left to right. Upon success, you hear a shutter sound.

Another technique is to press and hold the Power and Volume Down keys until you hear the shutter sound. This method is the most consistent way to capture the screen across all Android devices.

TECHNICAL STUFF

>> Screen shots are viewed in the Photos app along with other images you snap and videos you record.

>> Screen shots are kept in the DCIM/Screenshots folder in the tablet's internal storage. They're saved in the JPEG graphics file format.

Camera Settings and Options

The Camera app sports multiple features, some of which you'll probably never use. It's good to have variety, but without some advice, it's difficult to know which features are important and which you can play with later. This section lists many of the important features and options.

Setting the flash

To control the Galaxy Tab S4's rear camera flash, tap the Flash icon on the Camera app's screen. (Refer to Figure 12-1.) As you tap, the icon changes to represent one of three flash settings, illustrated in Table 12-1.

>> When recording video, the tablet's flash lamp is either on or off. Choose the Flash On icon before shooting to enable the lamp.

>> A good time to turn on the flash is when taking pictures of people or objects in front of something bright, such as a fuzzy brown kitten playing with a ball of white yarn in front of an exploding gasoline truck.

TABLE 12-1   ## Galaxy Tablet Camera Flash Settings

Setting	Icon	Description
Auto	⚡A	The flash activates during low-light situations but not when it's bright out.
On	⚡	The flash always activates.
Off	⚡̸	The flash never activates, even in low-light situations.

Changing still resolution and video quality

Too many people ignore the resolution and quality settings, not only on tablets but on digital cameras as well. Either that, or they just figure that the highest value is best. That's not always the case.

High-resolution images are ideal for printing pictures and for photo editing. They're not ideal for images you plan on sharing with Facebook or sending as email attachments. For video quality, the resolution should reflect the output device; low quality is fine for videos you plan on watching on the Tab.

Further, the higher-resolution images and high-quality videos occupy more storage space. Don't be disappointed when your tablet fills up with vacation photos because the resolution is too high.

Another problem with resolution is remembering to set it *before* you snap the photo. It's not that difficult!

 In the Camera app, tap the Settings icon. You see two categories, one for the rear camera and another for the front camera. Two items dwell in each category: Picture Size and Video Size. Tap the item you want to set.

For example, to adjust the rear camera's video quality, choose the Video Size option below the Rear Camera heading. Sizes are listed by crazy acronyms as well as by frame resolution. I would choose HD for videos I plan on sharing on social media. For stuff I want to edit, I'd choose UHD.

Tap the Back navigation icon when you're done setting resolution or quality. The next image you snap or video you record is created using the settings you've chosen.

TECHNICAL
STUFF

>> *Megapixel* is a measurement of the amount of information stored in an image. A megapixel is approximately 1 million *pixels,* or individual dots that compose an image.

>> Video quality uses these exciting acronyms: HD (High Definition), 1:1 (square), FHD (Full High Definition), QHD (Quad High Definition), and UHD (Ultra High Definition). I don't know if a superlative beyond *ultra* exists, but the technology industry will find it.

Activating the location tag

Your Galactic tablet's camera not only takes a picture but also keeps track of where you're located on Planet Earth when you take the picture. The feature is commonly called *geotag*, but in the Camera app it's known as Location Tags.

 To ensure that the geotag feature is enabled, or to disable the feature, tap the Settings icon in the Camera app. Swipe down the CAMERA SETTINGS screen to find the Location Tags item. Swipe the master control to On to activate or to Off to disable.

See Chapter 13 for information on using a photograph's location data.

Chapter **13**

All the Photos in Your Galaxy

There's no point in the Galaxy Tab having a camera unless it also has a place to store pictures and videos. That location is a digital Louvre of sorts, called the Photos app. It's more than just a point-at-the Picasso type of gallery because, in addition to looking at the painting of the woman with the weird eyeballs, you can use the Photos app to fix those eyes. Or, you can accept the eyeballs and flip to the next photo. The Photos app does it all.

A second app is also available for viewing photos and videos. It's Samsung's Gallery app, which is modeled after the original Android photo-and-video app. The Photos app hooks into your Google account, which is why I'm covering it here exclusively.

Your Pictures and Videos

The Photos screen, shown in the center in Figure 13-1, lists items by date. Tap the Photos icon at the bottom of the screen to ensure that this view is active.

Video

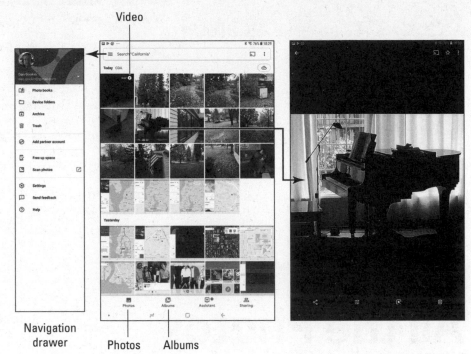

FIGURE 13-1:
Image
organization in
the Photos app.

Navigation
drawer

Photos   Albums

To see any photo albums, tap the Albums icon at the bottom of the screen. Albums are closely associated with your online photos accessed from your Google account, covered elsewhere in this chapter, so these could be albums created on another device that uses your same Google account.

To view an image, tap its thumbnail. You see the image appear full-screen, as shown on the right in Figure 13-1. Swipe the screen left or right to browse your images.

 Video thumbnails feature the Play icon, shown in the margin. Tap that icon to view the video. As the video is playing, tap the screen again to view the onscreen controls.

>> While you're viewing an image or a video full-screen, the navigation icons may disappear. Tap the screen to view them.

 >> Tap the Back navigation icon to return to an album after viewing an image or a video.

Creating an album

If you prefer to organize your images by album instead of by date, follow these steps in the Photos app:

1. **View an image you want to add to an album.**

   Ensure that the image is shown full-screen, as shown on the far right in Figure 13-1.

2. **Tap the Action Overflow.**

3. **Choose Add to Album.**

4. **Tap Album on the CREATE NEW card.**

   The image is added to a new, empty album.

5. **Type a name for the album.**

6. **Tap the Done icon to create the album and add the first image.**

To add more images to the album, repeat these steps, but choose the specific album in Step 4.

TIP

To add a swath of images to an album, long-press the first one. Continue tapping images to build up a group. Tap the Add (plus) icon, and choose the album from the list.

REMEMBER

To switch between Album mode and Photos mode, tap the proper icon at the bottom of the Photos app's main screen, as shown in Figure 13-1.

Starting a slideshow

The Photos app can display a slideshow of your images, but without the darkened room and sheet hanging over the mantle. To view a slideshow, follow these steps:

1. **View an image full-screen.**

2. **Tap the Action Overflow icon.**

3. **Choose Slideshow.**

   Images from that particular album or date appear one after the other on the screen.

Tap the Back navigation icon to exit the slideshow.

Slideshows don't have to remain in your Android. If a nearby HDMI TV or monitor features a Chromecast dongle, tap the Chromecast icon, shown in the margin. Choose a specific Chromecast gizmo from the list to view the slideshow on a larger screen. See Chapter 18 for more details on using Chromecast to stream media.

Finding a picture's location

Your tablet can be configured to save additional information with each picture you snap. Details are offered in Chapter 12. What you can do with that information is display it while viewing a picture, and even locate the exact spot where you took a picture, right on the Maps app.

To view location information for a photo, view the image full-screen and swipe down. Below the LOCATION heading, you see a map image of where the picture was taken. Tap the image to view the location in the Maps app. (Refer to Chapter 11 for details on the Maps app.)

TIP

>> The location information stays with the image, even if you share the photo on the Internet. To remove the information, you must obtain an image editing app from Google Play. Look for a JFIF editor or any app that removes location or geotag data from images.

>> Not every image stores location information. In some cases, the tablet cannot read its GPS radio to store the information. At other times, the feature is disabled. When this happens, location information is unavailable.

>> Refer to Chapter 12 for information on how to turn location information on or off when taking pictures.

Edit and Manage Images

The best tool for image editing is a computer armed with photo editing software, such as Photoshop or one of its less expensive alternatives. Even so, it's possible to use the Photos app to perform some minor photo surgery.

Editing an image

To enter Image Editing mode in the Photos app, view the image you want to modify and tap the Controls icon, shown in the margin. If you don't see this icon, tap the screen and it shows up.

Editing tools are presented in three categories, shown at the bottom of the screen and illustrated in Figure 13-2: preset effects, image settings, and crop/rotate.

>> The Preset Effects item presents a scrolling palette (swipe left-right) of options, each of which adjusts the image's tonal qualities.

>> The Image Settings control lets you adjust specific aspects of an image: light, color, and pop. A chevron by the Light and Color items provides more detailed image control.

>> The crop-and-rotate function is covered in the later sections "Cropping an image" and "Rotating a picture."

Action Overflow

Cancel edits.   Save changes.

Preset Effects   Image Settings   Crop/Rotate

FIGURE 13-2:
Image editing in
the Photos app.

Tap the Save button when you're done editing. This action replaces the image with your edited copy.

 Tap the Cancel button to discard your edits. Tap the DISCARD button to confirm.

Unediting an image

The changes you make to an image in the Photos app are directly applied to the image; an original copy isn't retained. To remove any previously applied edits, crops, or rotation effects, view the image in the Photos app and follow these steps:

1. **Tap the Edit icon to edit the image.**

2. **Tap the Action Overflow.**

3. **Choose Undo Edits.**

4. **Tap the Save button.**

The original image is restored.

Cropping an image

To *crop* an image is to snip away parts you don't want or need, similar to taking a pair of scissors to a photograph of you and your old girlfriend, though the process is far less cathartic. To crop an image, obey these steps:

1. **View the image in the Photos app.**

2. **Tap the Edit icon.**

3. **Tap the Crop / Rotate icon.**

   The icon is shown in the margin. The screen changes as illustrated in Figure 13-3. The tools that are presented crop and rotate the image.

4. **Drag any of the four corners to crop the image.**

   As you drag, portions of the image are removed.

   You can also drag the image within the cropping rectangle to modify the crop action.

   TIP

5. **Tap the Done button.**

   The image is cropped. You can continue to edit, or tap the Save button to make the changes permanent. (Refer to the earlier section "Editing an image.")

If you're unhappy with the changes after tapping the Done button, tap the Action Overflow and choose Undo Edits.

TIP

Use the Aspect Ratio icon (refer to Figure 13-3) to adjust the cropping box for the image to a new presentation, such as square or widescreen.

Cropping corners   Cropping rectangle   Cropping corners

FIGURE 13-3:
Rotating and
cropping an
image.

Set aspect ratio.   Set rotation angle.   90° tool

Rotating a picture

Showing someone else an image on a tablet can be frustrating, especially when the image is a vertical picture that refuses to fill the screen when the device is in a vertical orientation. To fix this issue, rotate the image in the Photos app. Follow these steps:

1. **Display the cockeyed image.**

2. **Tap the Edit icon.**

3. **Choose the Crop / Rotate tool.**

4. **Tap the 90° icon to rotate the image in 90-degree increments, or drag the sliders to set a specific angle.**

   Refer to Figure 13-3 for the location of these controls on the editing screen.

5. **Tap the Done icon to save the changes.**

   You can continue editing.

6. **Tap the Save button to make the changes permanent.**

Rotating an image to a specific angle also crops the image. This step is necessary to maintain the image's aspect ratio.

Editing video

The Photos app features limited options for editing recorded video. They are: trim the video, stabilize, and rotate.

 To edit a video, tap its thumbnail in the Photos app. As it plays, tap the Controls icon, shown in the margin. You see the video displayed for editing, as illustrated in Figure 13-4.

TIP

>> To trim the video, adjust the start and end trim controls, shown in Figure 13-4. Drag them to a new position to reset when the video starts and ends.

>> To assist you with your edits, swipe the video preview frames left and right. This scrubbing action helps to set the new starting and ending points for the movie.

>> Tap the Stabilize button to process the video for the removal of any undesired camera shaking.

>> To rotate the video, tap the Rotate button. Each time you tap, the video is rotated in 90-degree increments.

Cancel edits   Save button appears here

FIGURE 13-4: A video, primed for editing.

Video start trim control

Play head indicator

Video start trim control

When you're done editing, tap the Save button, which appears in the upper right corner of the screen (not shown in Figure 13-4). Tap the X (cancel) button to discard any edits. You may be prompted to confirm you want to discard the changes.

Deleting images and videos

It's entirely possible, and often desirable, to remove unwanted, embarrassing, or questionably legal images and videos from the Photos app.

 To banish something to the bit dumpster, tap the Delete (trash) icon on the screen when viewing an image or a video. To confirm, tap the Move to Trash button.

>> If you don't see the Delete icon, the item cannot be deleted. It's most likely a copy pulled in from a web photo-sharing service or a social networking site.

>> To view the Trash album, tap the Side Menu icon and choose Trash from the navigation drawer.

>> Items held in the Trash album are automatically deleted after 60 days. To hasten the departure, long-press items in the Trash album to select a hoard of them, and then tap the Delete icon atop the screen.

Set Your Pics and Vids Free

Keeping your precious moments and memories by themselves in the Tab is an elegant solution to the problem of lugging around photo albums and a video projector. When you want to show your pictures to the widest possible audience, you need a bigger stage. That stage is the Internet, and you have many ways to send and save your pictures and videos online, as covered in this section.

>> Refer to Chapter 18 for information on synchronizing and sharing information between the Galaxy Tab and a computer.

>> Refer to Chapter 18 also for information on printing pictures on your Tab.

Posting a video to YouTube

The best way to share a video is to upload it to YouTube. As a Google account holder, you also have a YouTube account. You can use the tablet's YouTube app to upload your videos to the Internet, where everyone can see them and make rude comments. Here's how:

1. **Ensure that the Wi-Fi connection is activated.**

The best way to upload a video is to turn on the Wi-Fi connection, which doesn't incur data surcharges as the mobile data network does.

2. **Open the Photos app.**

3. **View the video you want to upload.**

You do not need to play the video. Just have it on the screen.

4. **Tap the Share icon.**

If you don't see the Share icon, tap the screen.

5. **Choose YouTube.**

The Add Details card appears. You may first see a tutorial on trimming the video, which is the next step.

6. **Trim the video, if necessary, resetting the starting and ending points.**

If you opt to trim, drag the starting and ending points for the video left or right. As you drag, the video is scrubbed, allowing you to preview the start and end points.

7. **Type the video's title.**

8. **Type a description.**

The description appears on YouTube when people go to view the video.

9. **Set whether the video is private, public, or unlisted.**

A *private* video is viewable only by you or anyone you specifically invite to view it. A *public* video is viewable by everyone in the universe. An *unlisted* video is viewable by anyone to whom you share the video's link; it cannot be searched for in YouTube.

10. **Tap the Send icon.**

You return to the gallery, and the video is uploaded. The video continues to upload even if the tablet falls asleep.

When the upload has completed and the video is uploaded to YouTube, a notification appears. To view your video, open the YouTube app. It's found on the Apps screen and discussed in Chapter 15.

Sharing images with other apps

 Just about every app wants to get in on the sharing bit, especially when it comes to sharing pictures and videos. The key is to view something in the Photos app and then tap the Share icon, shown in the margin. From the Share card, choose an app, and that image or video is instantly sent to that app.

What happens next?

That depends on the app. For Facebook, Twitter, and other social networking apps, the image is attached to a new post. For Email or Gmail, the image or video becomes an attachment. Other apps treat the image in a similar manner: It's made available to the app for sharing, posting, sending, or what-have-you. The key is to look for that Share icon.

Chapter **14**

Music Everywhere

Your tablet's amazing arsenal of features includes its capability to play music. So it effectively replaces any gramophone that you've been lugging around, which is the whole idea behind an all-in-one gizmo like a Galaxy Tab. You can cheerfully and adeptly transfer all your old Edison cylinders and 78 LPs over to the tablet for your listening enjoyment. This chapter tells you how.

Your Hit Parade

The source of your musical joy on the Galaxy tablet is an app aptly named Play Music. You can find this app on the Apps screen. It might also dwell inside the Google folder on the Home screen.

» The first time you start the Play Music app, you may be asked whether you'd like to try Google Play Music All Access. It's an all-the-time music service from Google, available for a monthly fee. You do not have to subscribe to the service to use the Play Music app on your tablet.

» As with other Google services, music on your Android that's available through the Play Music app is also available online at play.google.com/music.

» See the later section "Soap, No Soap, Galaxy Radio" for details on streaming music apps.

Browsing your music library

The Play Music app lists music available on your tablet as well as music associated with your online Google account. To view your music library, obey these steps:

1. **Start the Play Music app.**

2. **Tap the Side Menu icon to display the navigation drawer.**

The Side Menu icon is found in the upper left corner of the screen. It's shown in the margin. If you see a left-pointing arrow instead, tap that arrow until the Side Menu icon appears.

3. **Choose Music Library.**

The Play Music app is shown in Figure 14-1 with the Music Library screen selected. Your music is organized by categories, which appear as tabs atop the screen. Switch categories by tapping a tab, or swipe the screen left or right to browse your music library.

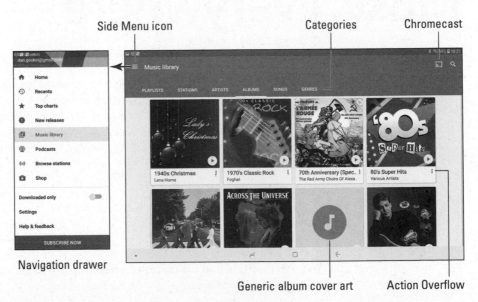

FIGURE 14-1:
The Music library.

The categories are merely ways the music is organized — ways to make the music easier to find when you may know, say, an artist's name but not an album title. The Genres category is for those times when you're in the mood for a certain type of music but don't know, or don't mind, who recorded it.

>> Is your Music Library empty or pathetically small? Get some music! See Chapter 16.

- » Songs and albums feature the Action Overflow icon, shown in the margin. Use that icon to view actions associated with the album or artist.

- » Two types of album artwork are used by the Play Music app. For purchased music, or music recognized by the app, original album artwork appears. Otherwise, the app shows a generic album cover.

- » When the Play Music app doesn't recognize an artist, it uses the title Unknown Artist. This happens with music you copy manually to your Tab, but it can also apply to audio recordings you make.

Playing a tune

After perusing your music library, select a tune to play: Tap a song to hear it. When you tap on an album, you see the list of individual songs, plus the large Play icon, shown in the margin. Tap this icon to listen to the entire album.

When the song plays, controls and other information appear at the bottom of the screen, as shown in Figure 14-2. Tap that strip to view full-screen controls.

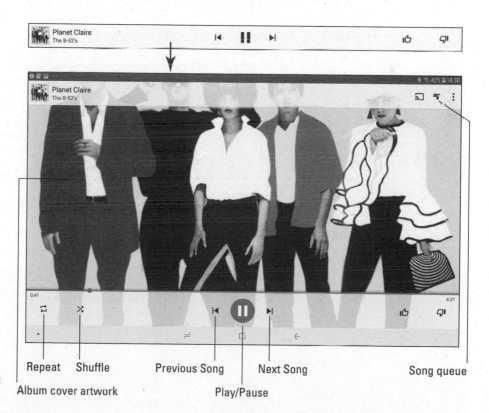

FIGURE 14-2:
A song is playing.

Repeat   Shuffle   Previous Song   Next Song   Song queue

Album cover artwork   Play/Pause

You're free to do other things while music plays on your Tab. You can even lock the screen and the music plays. Choose the Play Music notification, shown in the margin, to return to the Play Music app. While using the tablet, pull down the notifications panel and use the controls on the Play Music notification to pause the music or skip to the next or previous song. When the tablet is locked, music controls appear on the Lock screen.

After the song has finished playing, the next song in the list plays. The list order depends on how you start the song. For example, if you start a song from Album view, all songs in that album play in the order listed.

TABLE 14-1

Shuffle and Repeat Icons

Icon	Setting	What Happens When You Touch the Icon
	No Shuffle	Songs play one after the other.
	Shuffle	Songs are played in random order.
	No Repeat	Songs don't repeat.
	Single Repeat	The same song plays over and over.
	List Repeat	All songs in the list play over and over.

The next song in the list doesn't play if you have the Shuffle button activated. (Refer to Figure 14-2.) In that case, the Play Music app randomly chooses another song from the same list. Who knows which one will be next?

The next song might not play also when you have the Repeat option on: The three Repeat settings, as well as the Shuffle settings, are listed in Table 14-1. To change settings, tap the Shuffle icon or the Repeat icon.

To stop a song from playing, tap the Play/Pause icon.

REMEMBER

>> Use the tablet's volume button to set the volume.

>> Music in the Play Music app is streamed from the cloud. That means music doesn't play when an Internet connection is unavailable. See Chapter 16 for information on keeping music on the Tab.

>> To change the song order, tap the Song Queue icon, shown in Figure 14-2. You see a list of song cards in the order the songs play. Use the tab on the left side of each song card to change the order; drag the card up or down. Also see the section "Organize Your Music," later in this chapter.

>> You can use the Galaxy tablet's search capabilities to help locate tunes in your Music library. You can search by artist name, song title, or album. The key is to touch the Search icon when you're using the Play Music app. Type all or part of the text you're searching for, and then touch the Search button on the onscreen keyboard. Choose the song you want to hear from the list that's displayed.

>> When a song is playing or paused, its album artwork might appear as the Lock screen wallpaper. Don't let the change alarm you.

Queuing up the next song

It's fun to randomly listen to your music library, plucking out tunes like a mad deejay. Oftentimes, however, you don't have the patience to wait for the current song to finish before choosing the next tune. The solution is to add songs to the queue. Follow these steps:

1. Browse your music library for the next song (or album) you want to play.

2. Tap the song's Action Overflow.

3. Choose Add to Queue.

The Play Music app adds the song to the list of tunes to play next.

Songs are added to the queue in the order you tap them. That is, unless you instead choose the command Play Next in Step 3, in which case the tune is inserted at the top of the queue.

To review the queue, tap the Song Queue icon, shown in the margin as well as in Figure 14-2. Songs in the queue play in order, from the top down. To change the order, drag a song card up or down. To remove a song from the queue, swipe its card left or right.

TIP

If you like your queue, consider making a playlist of those same songs. See the section "Saving the song queue as a playlist," later in this chapter.

Being the life of the party

You need to do four things to make your Galaxy Tab the soul of your next shindig or soirée:

>> Connect it to external speakers.

>> Use the Shuffle command.

>> Set the Repeat command.

>> Provide plenty of drinks and snacks.

For external speakers, you can use anything from a custom media dock, a stereo, or the sound system on the Times Square Jumbotron. You need an audio cable with a mini-headphone plug on one end and an audio connector for the other device on the other end. Look for such a cable at any store where the employees wear name tags.

The Play Music app lets you cast music to a Chromecast device. Tap the Chromecast icon, shown in the margin as well as in Figure 14-1, to send your tunes to an HDTV or another Chromecast-connected output gizmo. See Chapter 18 for specific directions.

Enjoy your party, and please drink responsibly.

Organize Your Music

The Play Music app categorizes your music by album, artist, song, and so forth, but unless you have only one album and enjoy all the songs on it, that configuration probably won't do. To better organize your music, you can create *playlists*. That way, you can hear the music you want to hear, in the order you want, for whatever mood hits you.

Reviewing your playlists

To view any playlists that you've already created or that have been preset on the tablet, tap the Side Menu icon and choose Playlists from the list of categories shown atop the main Play Music app screen. (Refer to Figure 14-1.)

To see which songs are in a playlist, tap the Playlist icon. To play the songs in the playlist, tap the Play button.

Creating your own playlists

Making a new playlist is easy, and adding songs to the playlist is even easier. Follow these steps:

1. **Find an album or a song in the library.**

   Locate music you want to add to a playlist.

2. **Tap the Action Overflow icon and choose Add to Playlist.**

3. **Choose NEW PLAYLIST.**

4. **Type a name for the playlist.**

5. **Type a description.**

6. **Tap the CREATE PLAYLIST button.**

   The new playlist is created, and the song or entire album is added to the playlist.

To add songs, or to build upon an existing playlist, repeat Steps 1 and 3, but in Step 3 choose the existing playlist.

>> You can have as many playlists as you like on the tablet and stick as many songs as you like into them. Adding songs to a playlist doesn't noticeably affect the tablet's storage capacity.

>> To remove a song from a playlist, open the playlist, tap the Action Overflow icon next to the song, and choose Remove from Playlist.

>> Removing a song from a playlist doesn't delete the song from the Music library.

>> Songs in a playlist can be rearranged: While viewing the playlist, drag the tab on the far left end of a song title up or down in the list.

>> To delete a playlist, tap the playlist's Action Overflow icon. Choose Delete, and then tap OK to confirm.

Saving the song queue as a playlist

If you've created a song queue, and it's a memorable one, consider saving that queue as a playlist that you can listen to over and over. Obey these directions:

1. **Tap the Song Queue icon to view the song queue.**

   Refer to the earlier section "Queuing up the next song" for details on the song queue.

2. **Tap the Action Overflow icon next to the Song Queue icon.**

3. **Choose Save Queue.**

4. **Tap the NEW PLAYLIST button.**

   Or, you can add the songs to an existing playlist: Select the playlist from the Add to Playlist card.

5. **Fill in the New Playlist card with a name and description.**

6. **Tap the CREATE PLAYLIST button.**

The songs in the current queue now dwell in their own playlist, or have been added to an existing playlist. The queue's songs are now available from that playlist.

Removing unwanted music

To remove a song or an album, tap its Action Overflow icon. Choose the Delete command. Tap the OK button to remove the song. Bye-bye, music.

TIP

I don't recommend removing music. Most music on your Tab is actually stored in the cloud, in Google's Play Music service. Therefore, removing the music doesn't affect the tablet's storage. So, unless you despise the song or artist, removing the music has no effect.

See Chapter 16 for information on where music is stored, how to download it to the Tab, or other information.

Soap, No Soap, Galaxy Radio

Though they're not broadcast radio stations, some sources on the Internet — *Internet radio* sites — play music. Lamentably, the Galaxy Tab doesn't come with any Internet radio apps, but that doesn't stop you from finding a few good ones at Google Play. Some free services that I can recommend are

>> Pandora Radio

>> Spotify

>> TuneIn Radio

Pandora Radio and Spotify let you select music based on your mood and preferences. The more feedback you give the apps, the better the music selections.

The TuneIn Radio app gives you access to hundreds of Internet radio stations broadcasting around the world. They're organized by category, so you can find just about whatever you want. Many of the radio stations are also broadcast radio stations, so odds are good that you can find a local station or two, which you can listen to on your Galaxy Tab.

These apps are available at the Google Play Store. They're free, though paid versions might also be available.

WARNING

TECHNICAL STUFF

>> Google offers an unlimited music listening service. You can tap the item SUBSCRIBE NOW on the Play Music app's navigation drawer to sign up. The service is free for 30 days, and then a nominal fee, currently $9.99, is charged monthly.

>> It's best to listen to Internet radio when your tablet is connected to the Internet via a Wi-Fi connection. Streaming music can use a lot of your cellular data plan's data allotment.

>> See Chapter 16 for details on Google Play, though a shortcut exists in the Play Music app: From the Side Menu, choose the Shop action.

>> Internet music of the type delivered by the apps mentioned in this section is referred to by the nerds as *streaming music*. That's because the music arrives on your Galaxy tablet as a continuous download from the source. Unlike music you download and save, streaming music is played as it comes in and is not stored long-term.

Chapter **15**

What Else Does It Do?

Most gizmos are designed to solve a single problem. The food processor slices, grates, or chops food, but It doesn't play music (though I'm sure John Cage would argue that point). The lawn mower is good at cutting the grass but terrible at telling time. And if you have a tuba, it can play music, but it's a poor substitute for a hair dryer. That's all well and good because people accept limitations on devices designed with a specific purpose.

The Galaxy Tab is a gizmo with many purposes. Its capabilities are limited only by the apps installed. To help you grasp this concept, the tablet comes with a host of apps that can give you an idea of the tablet's capabilities. Or, you can simply use those apps to make the tablet a more versatile and useful device.

It's an Alarm Clock

Your Galaxy Tab keeps constant, accurate track of the time, which is displayed at the top of the Home screen as well as on the Lock screen. The display is lovely and informative, but it can't actually wake you up. You need to choose a specific time and apply a noise to that time. This process turns the tablet into an alarm clock.

Alarm clock duties are the responsibility of the Clock app. Its main screen features four tabs representing distinct chronological functions: alarm, world clock, stopwatch, and timer.

To set an alarm, heed these directions when using the Clock app:

1. **Tap the ALARM tab.**

2. **Tap the Add icon.**

   A card appears, which you use to set the alarm time, days, name, and so on.

3. **Fill in details about the alarm.**

   Set the alarm's time. Determine whether it repeats daily or only on certain days. Choose a ringtone. Ponder over any other settings as shown on the card. The alarm name appears when the alarm triggers.

4. **Tap the SAVE button.**

You can confirm that an alarm is set when you see the Alarm Set status icon atop the touchscreen, as shown in the margin.

When the alarm triggers, slide the Dismiss icon or press the Volume key. Some alarms may feature the Snooze icon. Tap it to be annoyed again after a few minutes.

REMEMBER

>> Alarms must be set to activate.

>> Your Galaxy Tab keeps its clock accurate by accessing an Internet time server. You never have to set the time.

>> Unsetting an alarm doesn't delete the alarm. To remove an alarm, long-press it and then tap the DELETE button.

>> To make the alarm sound on specific days of the week, use the Repeat option. Choose the days of the week when you want the alarm to sound. Otherwise, the alarm sounds only when you set it.

>> The alarm doesn't work when you turn off the tablet. The alarm may not sound when Do Not Disturb mode is active. The alarm does trigger when the touchscreen is locked.

>> So tell me: Do alarms go off, or do they go on?

It's a Very Big Calculator

The Calculator is perhaps the oldest of all computer programs. Even my stupid cellphone back in the 1990s had a Calculator program. (I won't dignify it by calling it an app.)

The Calculator app is shown in Figure 15-1. Tap various buttons to input equations. The Parentheses button helps set which part of a long equation gets calculated first. Use the C button to clear input.

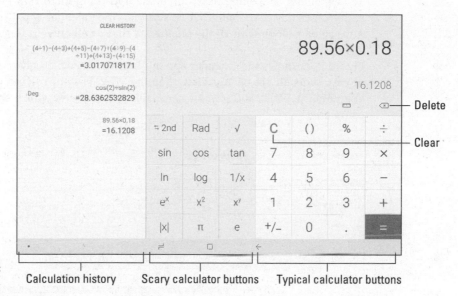

FIGURE 15-1:
The calculator.

Calculation history   Scary calculator buttons   Typical calculator buttons

TIP

» Long-press the calculator's text (or results) to cut or copy the results.

» I use the Calculator app most often to determine my tip at a restaurant. In Figure 15-1, a calculation is being made for an 18 percent tip on an $89.56 tab.

It's a Calendar

Toss out your old datebook. You never need to buy another one again. That's because your Tab is the ideal datebook and appointment calendar. Thanks to the Calendar app and the Google Calendar feature on the Internet, you can manage all your scheduling right on your Galaxy tablet. It's almost cinchy.

» You automatically have a Google Calendar; it comes with your Google account. You can visit Google Calendar on the web at `calendar.google.com` or use the Calendar app instead.

» Before you throw away your datebook, copy into the Calendar app some future appointments and info, such as birthdays and anniversaries.

Browsing your schedule

To see what's happening next, to peruse upcoming important events, or just to know which day of the month it is, summon the Calendar app. It's located on the Apps screen, along with all the other apps that dwell on your Galactic tablet.

Figure 15-2 shows the Calendar app in Month view, which gives a good overview of your schedule. To change views, tap the VIEW button. You can choose between Year, Month, Week, and Day. Also available is Tasks view, which shows tasks to be completed.

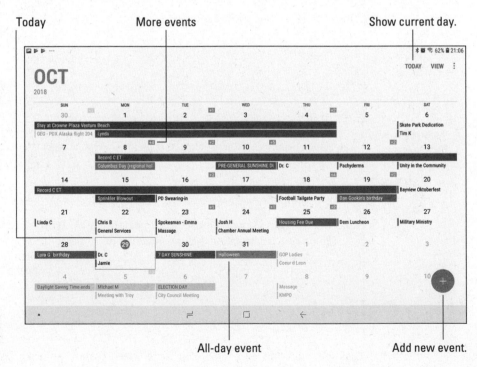

FIGURE 15-2: The Calendar app.

TIP

» I check Week view at the start of the week to remind me of what's coming up.

» To scroll from month to month, week to week, or day to day, swipe the screen left or right.

» Tap the TODAY button to be instantly whisked back to the current day.

» The current date, if it's visible on the screen, appears highlighted, as shown in Figure 15-3. In Week view and Day view, a horizontal red bar marks the current time.

» Different colors flag your events, as seen by the bars next to event names in Figure 15-2. The colors represent a calendar category to which the events are assigned. See the later section "Creating an event" for information on calendar categories.

Reviewing appointments

To see more detail about an event, touch it. When you're using Month view, touch the event's date to see Week view. Then choose the event again to see its details, similar to the event shown in Figure 15-3.

Remove this event.

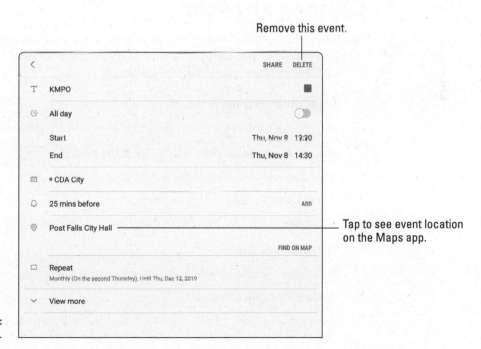

Tap to see event location on the Maps app.

FIGURE 15-3: Event details.

The details you see depend on how much information was recorded when the event was created. Some events have only a minimum of information; others may have details, such as a location for the event. When the event's location is listed, you can touch that location, and the Maps app pops up to show you where the event is being held.

 Tap the Back navigation icon to dismiss the event's details.

>> Birthdays and a few other events on the calendar may be pulled from the Contacts app or even from some social networking apps. That probably explains why some events are listed twice — they're pulled in from two sources.

>> To quickly view upcoming events from the Home screen, slap down the Calendar widget. See Chapter 19 for information on applying widgets to the tablet's Home screen.

>> The Google app also lists any immediate appointments or events. See the later section "It's Your Pal, Google."

Creating an event

The key to making the Calendar app work is to add events: appointments, things to do, meetings, or full-day events such as birthdays or colonoscopies. To create an event, follow these steps in the Calendar app:

1. **Select the day for the event.**

   This approach works best when using the Calendar app in Week view.

2. **Tap the approximate time on the day of the event.**

   The hour grows a rectangle with an Add (+) icon.

3. **Tap the Add (+) icon.**

   A new event card appears.

4. **Type an event title.**

   Sometimes I simply write the name of the person I'm meeting.

5. **Confirm the date and time.**

   If you followed Steps 1 and 2, this information is already set. You can make adjustments as necessary; tap the Start or End date and time to be precise.

6. **Choose an event calendar or a calendar category.**

Do not choose My Calendars or the Device calendar. If you do, the event won't be synchronized with your Google account and other devices.

7. **Set a reminder.**

The reminder arrives in the form of a notification, alerting you to the impeding event.

8. **Type a location for the event.**

My advice is to type information in the event's Location field just as though you're typing information to search for in the Maps app. When the event is displayed, the location is a link; tap the link to see where it is on a map.

9. **Set additional options.**

One of the most important options is Repeat, which is useful for creating scheduled events such as regular meetings, sports events, lessons, and other weekly or monthly occasions.

10. **Tap the SAVE button to create the new event.**

To change the event after creating it, tap the event on the Calendar app screen. You see a card, similar to what's shown in Figure 15-3. All fields are instantly open for editing. Tap the SAVE button to update the event.

To remove an event, tap the DELETE button on its card. (Refer to Figure 15-3.) Tap the DELETE button to confirm.

REMEMBER

>> The more information you supply, the more detailed the event and the more you can do with it on your tablet as well as on Google Calendar on the Internet.

>> It's necessary to set an event's time zone only when that event takes place in another time zone or when an event spans time zones, such as an airline flight. In that case, the Calendar app automatically adjusts the starting and stopping times for events, depending on where you are.

>> If you forget to set the time zone and you end up hopping around the world, your events are set according to the time zone in which they were created, not the local time.

>> Event reminders appear as notification icons (shown in the margin), as audio alerts, or as vibrating alerts. To peruse pending events, pull down the notifications and choose the calendar alert.

>> Calendar categories are handy because they let you organize and color-code your events. They're confusing because Google calls them calendars. I think of them more as categories. So I have different calendars (categories) for my personal and work schedules, government duties, clubs, and so on.

Adding a task

A task is different from a calendar event in that it has no specific duration — merely a due date. To set a task, such as a reminder to clean the gutters, obey these steps in the Calendar app:

1. **Tap the VIEW button and choose Tasks.**

2. **Tap the Add icon.**

3. **Type a title for the task.**

   Gotta eliminate that pile of detritus in the back yard.

4. **Type a due date, the day by which you desire to complete the task.**

   Gotta eliminate that pile of detritus in the back yard before the snow flies.

5. **Add a reminder.**

   This setting is necessary only when you lack a spouse who would otherwise remind you to complete the task. Unlike with the due date, you can set a specific time for the reminder.

6. **Tap the SAVE button to set the task.**

Tasks you create appear in the Calendar app's Task view. When you've completed the task — well before the reminder rings — tap the box by the task's title to mark it done. Completed tasks appear in the list with a satisfying line drawn through them. Tap the DELETE ALL button to remove completed tasks; tap DELETE to confirm.

It's an eBook Reader

The Galaxy Tab comes with Google's own eBook reader app, Play Books. It's found on the Apps screen, or you might find a launcher icon on the Home screen or in the Home screen's Google folder.

Begin your reading experience by opening the Play Books app. You may see the page of the last eBook you were reading. If not, you can view your entire book library: Tap the Library icon at the bottom of the page. The library lists any titles you've obtained for your Google Play Books account, similar to what's shown in Figure 15-4.

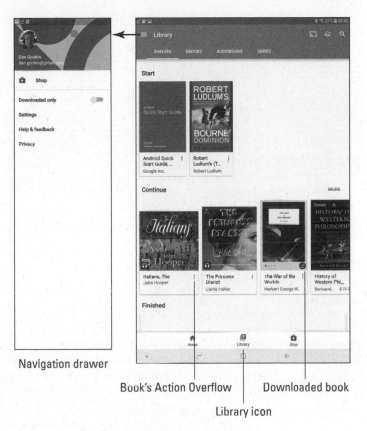

Navigation drawer

Book's Action Overflow   Downloaded book

Library icon

FIGURE 15-4: The Play Books library.

Scroll through your library by swiping the screen.

Tap a book's cover to open it. If you've opened the book previously, you're returned to the page you last read. Otherwise, you see the book's first page.

Figure 15-5 illustrates the basic book reading operation in the Play Books app. You turn pages by swiping the screen from right to left, assuming that you're reading English or other languages that read in that direction.

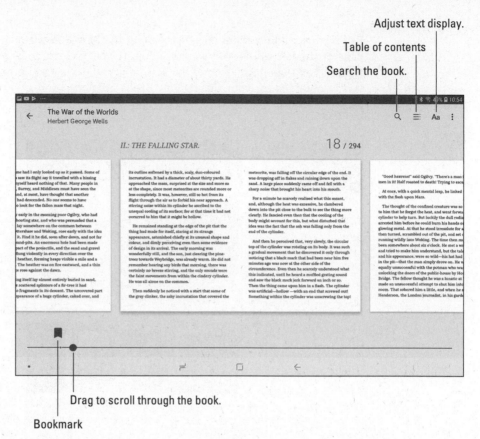

Adjust text display.

Table of contents

Search the book.

FIGURE 15-5:
Reading an
eBook in the
Play Books app.

Drag to scroll through the book.

Bookmark

The Play Books app also works in both vertical and horizontal orientations. You can lock the screen: Tap the Action Overflow and choose Settings to use the Auto-Rotate Screen item to select how you want the screen locked.

>> Books in your Play Books library are stored on the Internet and available to read only when an Internet connection is active. It's possible to keep a book on your Tab by downloading it to the device. Refer to Chapter 16 for details on downloading books.

>> To remove a book from the library, tap the Action Overflow icon on the book's cover and then choose the Delete from Library command.

>> If the onscreen controls (refer to Figure 15-5) disappear, tap the screen to see them again.

» Tap the Aa icon to display a menu of options for adjusting the text on the screen and the brightness.

» Unlike dead tree books, eBooks lack an index. That's because text on digital pages can change based on the book's presentation. Therefore, use the Search icon (refer to Figure 15-5) to look for items in the text.

» A copy of your eBook library is available on all your Android devices and on the Play Books website:

```
play.google.com/books
```

» Refer to Chapter 16 for information on obtaining books from Google Play.

» If you have a Kindle (and for that I must ask "Why?" — but I digress), you can obtain the Amazon Kindle app for your Tab. Use the app to access books you've purchased for the Kindle or just as a supplement to Google Books.

It's a Game Machine

For all its technology, the Galaxy Tab is keenly adept at amusing you through the abundant application of games. If no games come preinstalled on your Tab, you can eagerly hunt down some at Google Play, just like everyone else in the Android Kingdom: See Chapter 16 for details on using the Play Store app to browse for and obtain entertaining, challenging, or classic games for your tablet.

Free or "lite" versions of popular games exist. Before plunking down your hard-earned 99 cents, consider testing the free version.

TIP

It's Your Pal, Google

Don't worry about your Galaxy Tab controlling too much of your life: The tablet harbors no insidious intelligence, and the Robot Uprising is still years away. Until then, you can use your tablet's listening capabilities to enjoy a type of artificial intelligence called Google Assistant. It's like having your own, personal Jeeves, but without a retirement or health care plan.

Your Google Assistant dwells in an app titled Google. It can also be accessed from a Google widget that you may find affixed to the Tab's Home screen. Tap that widget, open the Google app, or utter "Okay, Google" to access your digital pal. You may need to work through some setup, but eventually the Assistant is ready to assist you.

As you use Google Assistant, its screen populates with information cards relative to that interest. To see more cards, keep using the app. Ask it questions (see the nearby sidebar, "Barking orders to your Google Assistant"), use it as you would use Google to search the Internet, or just browse the categories.

>> You cannot manually add cards to the Google Assistant screen. The best way to get more cards to show up is to use the app to search for items of interest.

>> Samsung also offers its own personal assistant app, Bixby. The Tab's far left Home screen page is where you'll find Bixby. It does many of the things that Google Assistant does, though not as well. Further, you must have a Samsung account to use Bixby.

BARKING ORDERS TO YOUR GOOGLE ASSISTANT

You can speak simple search terms to Google Assistant, such as "Find pictures of the pope." Or, you can give more complex orders, among them:

- Will it rain tomorrow?

- What time is it in Frankfurt, Germany?

- How many euros equal $25?

- What is 103 divided by 6?

- How can I get to Disneyland?

- Where is the nearest Canadian restaurant?

- What's the score of the Lakers–Celtics game?

- What is the answer to life, the universe, and everything?

When asked such questions, Google Assistant responds with a card as well as a verbal reply. When a verbal reply isn't available, Google search results are displayed.

It's Your Video Entertainment

It's not possible to watch "real" TV on your Tab, but a few apps come close. The YouTube app is handy for watching random, meaningless drivel, which I suppose makes it a lot like TV. Then there's the Play Movies & TV app, which lets you buy and rent real movies and TV shows from the Google Play Store. And when you tire of those apps, you can use the Camera app with its front-facing camera to pretend that you're the star of your own reality TV show.

>> Other video entertainment apps include the popular Netflix, Hulu, and HBO Now, and the list is pretty long. Many broadcast channels feature their own apps.

>> Also see Chapter 18 for information on screencasting video entertainment from your Android's diminutive screen to a humongous HDTV or monitor.

Enjoying YouTube

YouTube is the Internet phenomenon that proves that real life is indeed too boring and random for television. Or is that the other way around? Regardless, you can view the latest videos on YouTube — or contribute your own — by using the YouTube app on your Galactic tablet.

To search for videos in the YouTube app, tap the Search icon. Type the video name, a topic, or any search terms to locate videos. Zillions of videos are available.

The YouTube app displays suggestions for any channels you're subscribed to, which allows you to follow favorite topics or YouTube content providers.

REMEMBER

>> Use the YouTube app to view YouTube videos, rather than use the Chrome app to visit the YouTube website.

>> Ensure that the tablet is oriented horizontally to view the video in a larger size.

>> Not all YouTube videos are available for viewing on mobile devices.

Buying and renting movies

Google would prefer that you use its Play Movies & TV app to watch both purchased and rented videos on your Tab. Open the app and choose the video from the main screen. Items you've purchased show up in the app's library; tap the Library icon at the bottom center of the screen.

>> The actual renting or purchasing is done in the Play Store app. Check that app often for freebies and discounts. More details for renting and purchasing movies and shows are found in Chapter 16.

>> Any videos you've purchased from Google Play are available on the Internet for anytime viewing. Visit

```
play.google.com/movies
```

Chapter **16**

The Google Play Store

The place to find more stuff for your Galaxy Tab is the digital marketplace known as Google Play. You can obtain music, books, movies, TV shows, and, most importantly, apps. A lot of the stuff that's available is free. Some of it costs money, but not as much as you would expect. Bottom line: The Google Play Store is the place to go when you need to expand upon your Tab's capabilities.

Welcome to the Store

Google Play may sound like a place to go for buying nerdy children's outerwear, but it's really an online bazaar where you pick up new goodies for your tablet: apps, games, music, magazines, movies, TV shows, and books. You can browse, you can get free stuff, or you can pay. It all happens at the Play Store.

» Though it's called Google Play, the app is titled Play Store. These terms are used interchangeably.

» You obtain items from Google Play by *downloading* them from the Internet to your tablet. This file transfer works best at top speeds; therefore:

TIP

>> If you have an LTE Tab, I highly recommend that you connect it to a Wi-Fi network if you plan to obtain apps, books, or movies at Google Play. Wi-Fi not only gives you speed but also helps you avoid data surcharges. See Chapter 17 for details on connecting your tablet to a Wi-Fi network.

>> The Play Store app is frequently updated, so its look may change from what you see in this chapter.

Browsing Google Play

To access Google Play, open the Play Store app. A launcher icon for the Play Store app might also be available on the Home screen; otherwise, look on the Apps screen.

After opening the Play Store app, you see the main screen, similar to the one shown in Figure 16–1. If not, tap the Left Arrow icon in the upper left corner of the screen until you see the main screen. Or, if you see the Side Menu icon (shown in the margin), tap it and choose Home from the navigation drawer.

Side Menu icon   Search   Categories

Navigation drawer

Suggestions

FIGURE 16-1:
Google Play.

To browse, tap a category atop the screen. Available categories include apps, games, movies, TV shows, music, books, and magazines. For example, to browse for an app, you choose the Home category and then Top Charts to see what's hot. Further categories, such as Top Free Apps, help you refine your search.

TIP

When you have an idea of what you want, such as an app's name or even what it does, searching works fastest: Touch the Search (magnifying glass) icon at the top of the Play Store screen. (Refer to Figure 16-1.) Type all or part of the app's name or perhaps a description.

To see more information about an item, touch it to view a detailed description, screen shots, a video preview, comments, plus links to similar items, as shown in Figure 16-2.

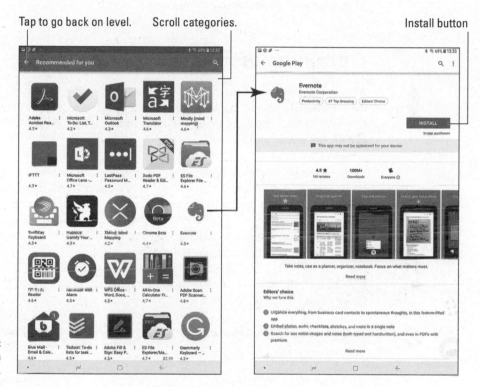

FIGURE 16-2: Hunting down an app.

>> The first time you enter Google Play, or immediately after an upgrade, you have to accept the terms of service; tap the ACCEPT button.

>> You can be assured that all apps that appear in Google Play can be used with your Galaxy Tab. There's no way to download or buy something that's incompatible.

>> Pay attention to an app's ratings. Ratings are added by people who use the apps — people like you and me. Having more stars is better. You can see additional information, including individual user reviews, by selecting the app.

TECHNICAL STUFF

>> Another good indicator of an app's success is how many times it's been downloaded. Some apps have been downloaded 100 million times. That's a good sign.

>> In Figure 16-2, the app's description (on the right) shows the INSTALL button. Other buttons that may appear on an app's description screen include OPEN, UPDATE, and UNINSTALL. The OPEN button opens an app that's already installed on the tablet; the UPDATE button updates an already installed app; and the UNINSTALL button removes an installed app. See Chapter 19 for more information on app management.

Obtaining an item

After you locate something you want from Google Play, the next step is to download it; the app, music, book, or movie is copied from Google Play on the Internet to your Galactic tablet. Apps are installed immediately. Books, music, and movies become available at once.

Good news: Most apps are available for free. Electronic versions of classic books are free. Occasionally, free movies and music are offered. Even when you pay for something, the cost isn't outrageous. The goal is to build your Tab's media library.

TIP

I recommend that you download a free app or eBook first, to familiarize yourself with the process. Then try your hand at a paid app.

Free or not, the process of obtaining an app works pretty much the same. Follow these steps:

1. **Ensure that the Tab is connected to the Internet on a Wi-Fi network.**

   You want to avoid mobile data surcharges for an LTE Tab.

2. **Open the Play Store app.**

3. **Find the item you want and open its description.**

   The description screen looks similar to the one shown on the right side in Figure 16-2, even for eBooks, music, and movies.

4. **Tap the button to obtain the item.**

   A free app features an INSTALL button. A free eBook features an EBOOK FREE button. For a free movie or TV show or music, look for a FREE button. You might also see a FREE SAMPLE or FREE TRIAL button for some items. In that case, tap the button to view or listen to a free sample of the media.

Paid items feature a button that shows the price. For movies and TV shows, you may see a Rent or Purchase button. See the later section "Renting or purchasing videos."

5. **Tap the Accept button, if prompted.**

The Accept button appears on an access card. It describes which device features the app uses. The list isn't a warning, just a summary. Even so, you're prompted later as the app runs and it requests permission to access various items.

6. **For a paid item, tap the Buy button.**

See the next section for further details on purchasing items at Google Play.

7. **Wait for the item to download or to become available.**

Media items are available instantly. Apps are downloaded and installed, which may take some time. Feel free to do something else while the app downloads. Installation takes place automatically.

8. **Tap the OPEN, PLAY, LISTEN, READ, or similar button to run the app, watch a video, listen to music, or read a book, respectively.**

Media arrives quickly to your Tab because it's not actually copied to the device. Instead, the item is *streamed*, or made available only when you request it. This process works as long as an Internet connection is available. See the later section "Keeping stuff on the device" for information on accessing media when an Internet connection isn't available.

>> The Play Store app prompts you for payment information if you haven't yet supplied it. This prompt appears even for free items, in which case you can skip the prompt: Tap the SKIP button. You can always supply payment information the first time you actually buy something.

>> If you chose to do something else while an app downloads, refer to the status bar to check for the Successfully Installed notification, shown in the margin. Choose that notification to open the recently obtained app.

>> Apps you download are added to the Apps drawer, made available like any other app on your phone or tablet. Additionally, you may find the app on the Home screen. See Chapter 20 for information on removing the app's launcher from the Home screen, if that is your desire.

>> Media you've obtained from Google Play is accessed from a specific app: Play Music for music, Play Books for books, and Play Movies & TV for video. Other chapters in this part of the book offer details.

>> After obtaining an item from Google Play, you receive a Gmail message confirming your purchase, paid or free.

>> See Chapter 20 for information on uninstalling apps.

>> Google Play doesn't currently offer refunds on purchased media, which includes music, books, and movies.

>> Keep an eye out for special offers from Google Play. These offer a great way to pick up some free songs, movies, and books.

TIP

Purchasing something at Google Play

When you purchase something at Google Play, you tap the Buy button. A card appears, listing available payment methods, similar to what's shown in Figure 16-3.

Current payment method

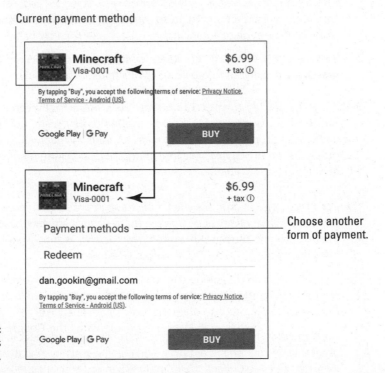

FIGURE 16-3: Google Play's Buy card.

In the figure, the app cost $6.99. The chosen payment method is a VISA card, though if you tap this item, you see more options for making the purchase. The selected payment method is used automatically after the Buy button is tapped. Here's how that operation works:

1. **Tap the BUY button.**

   For security, you're prompted to type your Google password.

2. **Type your Google password.**

   I strongly recommend that you *do not* choose the option Never Ask Me Again. You want to be prompted every time for your password.

WARNING

3. **Tap the Confirm button.**

4. **Type the credit card's security code.**

   This is the CVC code, found on the back of the card.

5. **Tap the VERIFY button.**

   The app is downloaded or the media made available to your phone or tablet.

To select another payment method, choose Payment Methods (refer to Figure 16-3) and select another credit or debit card or use your Google Play balance. After another payment method is selected, continue with Step 1 in this section.

>> Information about any potential refund is provided in the Gmail message you receive after the purchase. Review the message for details.

>> Be quick on that refund: For a purchased app, you have only two hours to get your money back. You know when the time limit is up, because the REFUND button on the app's description screen changes to UNINSTALL.

>> The credit or debit cards listed in Google Play are those you've used before. Don't worry: Your information is safe.

>> All music sales are final. Don't blame me; I'm just writing down Google's current policy for music purchases.

Renting or purchasing videos

When it comes to movies and TV shows available at the Google Play Store, you have two options: Rent or purchase.

When you desire to rent a video, the rental is available to view for the next 30 days. Once you start watching, however, you have only 24 hours to finish — you can also watch the video over and over again during that time span.

NEVER BUY ANYTHING TWICE

Any apps, music, books, or other items you buy from Google Play are yours as long as you keep your Google account or until the Robot Uprising, whichever comes first. That means that you don't have to buy anything — apps, music, books, videos — a second time.

For example, if you have an Android phone and you already paid for a slew of apps, you can obtain those same apps for your Galaxy Tab: Just visit Google Play and install the apps. The same rule goes for music, books, or anything you've previously paid for.

To review already purchased apps in Google Play, choose the My Apps & Games item in the sidebar. (Refer to Figure 16-1, on the left.) Choose the LIBRARY tab to see all the items you've ever obtained at Google Play, including stuff you've previously paid for. Select an item to reinstall the paid app.

Purchasing a video is more expensive than renting it, but you can view the movie or TV show at any time, on any Android device. You can also download the movie so that you can watch it even when an Internet connection isn't available, as described in the later section "Keeping stuff on the device."

One choice you must make when buying a movie is whether to purchase the SD or HD version. The SD version is cheaper and occupies less storage space (if you choose to download the movie). The HD version is more expensive, but it plays at high-definition only on certain output devices. Obviously, when watching on your Tab only, the SD option is preferred.

>> See Chapter 16 for information on the Play Movies app.

>> Also see Chapter 18 for information on casting videos from your Tab to a large-screen device, such as an HDTV.

Google Play Tricks

You may have no desire to be a Google Play expert. Just get the app you want, grouse over having to pay 99 cents for that must-have game or $4.99 to rent the latest blockbuster, and get on with your life. When you're ready to get more from the Play Store, peruse some of the items in this section.

Using the wish list

While you dither over getting a paid app, music, book, or any other purchase at the Play Store, consider adding it to your wish list: Tap the Wish List icon (shown in the margin) when viewing the app.

To review your wish list, tap the Side Menu icon in the Play Store app. (Refer to Figure 16-1.) Choose the My Wishlist item from the navigation drawer. You'll see all the items you've flagged. When you're ready to buy, choose one and buy it!

Sharing a Google Play item

Sometimes you love your Google Play purchase so much that you just can't contain your glee. When that happens, consider sharing the item. Obey these steps:

1. **Open the Play Store app.**

2. **Browse or search for the app, music, book, or other item you want to share.**

3. **When you find the item, tap it to view its description screen.**

4. **Tap the Share icon.**

   You may have to swipe down the screen to locate the Share icon, shown in the margin. After tapping the Share icon, you see a menu listing various apps.

5. **Choose an app.**

   For example, choose Gmail to send a Play Store link in an email message.

6. **Use the chosen app to send the link.**

   What happens next depends on which sharing method you've chosen.

The result of these steps is that your friend receives a link. That person can touch the link on his mobile Android gizmo and be whisked instantly to Google Play, where the item can be obtained.

Methods for using the various items on the Share menu are found throughout this book.

Keeping stuff on the device

Books, music, movies and TV shows you obtain from Google Play aren't copied to your Galaxy Tab. Instead, they're stored on the Internet. When you access the media, it's streamed into your tablet as needed. This setup works well, and it keeps your Tab from running out of storage space, but it works only when an Internet connection is available.

When you plan to be away from an Internet connection, such as when you're flying cross-country and are too cheap to pay for inflight Wi-Fi, you can download media purchases and save them on your tablet.

To see which media is on your Tab and which isn't, open the Play Books, Play Music, or Play Movies & TV app. Follow these steps, which work the same in each app:

1. **Tap the Side Menu icon.**

2. **In the navigation drawer, slide the master control by the Downloaded Only option to the On position.**

Just tap the gizmo and it toggles between On and Off settings.

3. **Choose the Library item from the navigation drawer.**

You see only those items on your tablet. The rest of your library, you can assume, is located on the Internet.

Repeat these steps to reset the Downloaded Only option to Off so that you can see all your books, music, and videos.

 Items downloaded to your tablet feature the On Device icon, similar to the one shown in the margin. The icon's color changes, depending on which app you're using.

 To keep an item on your tablet, look for the Download icon, shown in the margin. Tap that icon, and the item is fetched from the Internet and stored on your device.

 Keeping movies and lots of music on your Galaxy Tab consumes a lot of storage space. That's okay for short trips and such, but for the long term, consider purging some of your downloaded media: Tap the On Device icon. Tap the REMOVE button to confirm.

WARNING

Removing a downloaded item from your Tab doesn't delete it or prevent you from accessing it once an Internet connection is available. And you can download the movie, music, or book again and again without penalty or wrath.

4
Nuts and Bolts

Chapter **17**

It's a Wireless Life

What exactly is *portable?* Back in the olden days, the boys in Marketing would say that bolting a handle to just about anything made it portable. Even a rhinoceros would be portable if he had a handle. Well, and the legs, they kind of make the rhino portable, I suppose. But my point is that to be portable requires more than just a handle; it requires a complete lack of wires.

Your Samsung Galaxy Tab's battery allows it to wander away from a wall socket. The digital cellular signal offers Internet access pretty much all over. Other types of wireless communications are available, including Wi-Fi and Bluetooth. These features ensure portability.

Wireless Networking Wizardry

You know that wireless networking has hit the big-time when you see kids asking Santa Claus for a Wi-Fi router at Christmas. Such a thing would have been unheard of years ago because back then routers were used primarily for woodworking. Today, wireless networking is what keeps a gizmo such as your Galaxy Tab connected to the Internet.

Using the mobile data network

The LTE Tab uses the mobile data network to connect to the Internet, the same network type used by smartphones. Several types of digital cellular networks are available:

>> **4G LTE:** The fourth generation of wide-area data network and the fastest.

>> **3G:** The third-generation network, which is the fastest network when a 4G signal isn't available.

>> **1X:** The original, *slo-o-ower* cellular data signals, many of which are still available.

An LTE tablet always uses the best network available. So if the 4G LTE network is within reach, that network is used for Internet access. Otherwise, the 3G network is chosen next, and then 1X in an act of last-ditch desperation.

WARNING

>> A notification icon for the type of network being used appears in the status area, right next to the Signal Strength icon.

>> Accessing the digital cellular network isn't free. Your tablet most likely has some form of subscription plan for a certain quantity of data. When you exceed that quantity, the costs can become prohibitive.

>> See Chapter 22 for information on how to avoid cellular data overcharges when taking your Galaxy Tab out and about.

>> Also see Chapter 24 for information on monitoring your mobile data usage.

Understanding Wi-Fi

The digital cellular connection is nice, and it's available pretty much all over, but it costs you moolah. A better option, and one you should seek out when it's available, is *Wi-Fi*, or the same wireless networking standard used by computers for communicating with each other and the Internet.

Making Wi-Fi work on your Galactic tablet requires two steps. First, you must activate the tablet's Wi-Fi radio. Second, you connect the tablet to a specific wireless network. The next two sections cover both of these steps.

TECHNICAL STUFF

Wi-Fi stands for *wireless fidelity*. It's brought to you by the numbers 802.11 and various letters of the alphabet.

Activating and deactivating Wi-Fi

Follow these carefully written directions to activate Wi-Fi networking on your Galaxy Tab:

1. **Open the Settings app.**

   The app is found on the Apps screen, or you can use the shortcut on the Notifications shade.

2. **Choose Connections.**

3. **Ensure that the master control by the Wi-Fi setting is on.**

To disable the Wi-Fi radio, repeat these steps but set the master control to the Off position. Turning off Wi-Fi disconnects the tablet from any wireless networks.

And now, the shortcut: Pull down the notifications shade and use the Wi-Fi Quick Setting to turn Wi-Fi on or off. When the icon is highlighted, the Wi-Fi radio is on.

TIP

>> When activated, the Tab connects automatically to any known Wi-Fi networks. So, when you saunter back to the same café, the connection is established automatically.

>> Using Wi-Fi to connect to the Internet doesn't incur data usage charges.

REMEMBER

Connecting to a Wi-Fi network

After you've activated the tablet's Wi-Fi radio, you can connect to an available wireless network. Heed these steps:

1. **Open the Settings app.**

2. **Choose Connections tab.**

3. **On the right side of the screen, choose Wi-Fi.**

4. **Choose a wireless network from the list.**

   Available Wi-Fi networks appear on the right side of the screen, as shown in Figure 17-1. (As shown in the figure, I chose Imperial Wambooli, which is my office network.) When no wireless networks are listed, you're out of luck regarding wireless access from your current location.

5. **If the network requires a password, type it.**

   Tap the Enter Password text box to summon the onscreen keyboard.

   Tap the Show Password button to see what you're typing; some of those network passwords are *long*.

TIP

6. **Tap the CONNECT button.**

   The Tab is immediately connected to the network. If not, try the password again.

Signal strength   Password-protected network

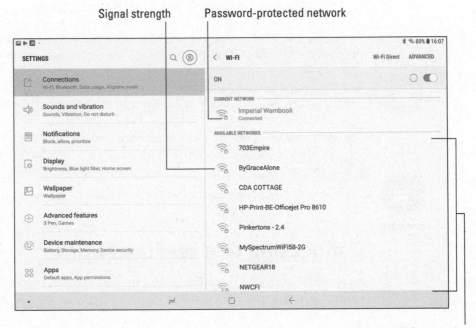

FIGURE 17-1:
Finding a wireless network.

Available Wi-Fi networks

When the Tab is connected to a wireless network, you see the Wi-Fi status icon, shown in the margin. This icon indicates that the tablet's Wi-Fi is on, connected, and communicating with the network.

>> Some public networks are open to anyone, but you must use the web browser app to access a login page before you're granted full access: Open the web browser app, browse to any page on the Internet, and the login page shows up.

>> To remember a Wi-Fi network, and automatically reconnect the next time your Tab is in range, tap the Auto Reconnect option when typing the network

password. (Refer to Step 5 in this section.) That way, you need not retype the password the next time the tablet uses that network.

WARNING

» Not every wireless network has a password. They should! Generally speaking, I don't avoid connecting to any public network that lacks a password, but I don't use that network for shopping, banking, or any other online activity that should be conducted securely.

» To disconnect from a Wi-Fi network, turn off the tablet's Wi-Fi radio. Refer to the preceding section.

TECHNICAL STUFF

» Unlike a cellular data network, a Wi-Fi network's broadcast signal goes only so far. My advice is to use Wi-Fi whenever you plan to remain in one location for a while. If you wander too far, your tablet loses the signal and is disconnected.

Connecting to a hidden Wi-Fi network

Some wireless networks don't broadcast their names, which adds security but also makes connecting more difficult. In these cases, choose the Add Network option located at the bottom of the list of available Wi-Fi networks. (Refer to Figure 17-1.) Type the network name, or *SSID*, and choose the type of security. You also need the password if one is used. You can obtain this information from the person in charge of the wireless network at your location, such as the girl with the nose ring who sold you coffee.

Connecting to a WPS router

Many Wi-Fi routers feature WPS, which stands for Wi-Fi Protected Setup. It's a network authorization system that's fast and quite secure. If the wireless router uses WPS and you can find the WPS icon shown in the margin, you can use this feature to quickly connect your Tab to the network.

To make a WPS connection, obey these steps:

1. **Open the Settings app and tap the Connections tab.**

2. **Choose Wi-Fi.**

3. **Tap the ADVANCED button.**

4. **Choose WPS Push Button for a push-button router, or choose WPS PIN Entry if the router requires you to type a PIN.**

   Follow the onscreen directions to complete the connection.

The Bluetooth Experience

Computer nerds have long had the desire to connect high-tech gizmos. The Bluetooth standard was developed to sate this desire in a wireless way. Though Bluetooth is wireless *communication*, it's not the same as wireless networking. It's more about connecting peripheral devices, such as keyboards, mice, printers, headphones, and other gear. It all happens in a wireless way, and it really has nothing to do with the color blue or anything dental.

Understanding Bluetooth

To make Bluetooth work, you need a Bluetooth peripheral, such as a wireless keyboard. The idea is to pair that peripheral with your tablet. The operation works like this:

1. **Turn on the Bluetooth wireless radio for both the Tab and the peripheral.**

2. **Make the peripheral discoverable.**

The gizmo is saying, "Hey! I'm over here!" Well, it's saying so electronically.

3. **On your tablet, choose the peripheral from the list of Bluetooth devices.**

4. **If necessary, confirm the connection.**

For example, you may be asked to type a code or press a button on the peripheral.

5. **Use the Bluetooth peripheral.**

You can use the Bluetooth peripheral as much as you like. Turn off the tablet. Turn off the peripheral. When you turn both on again, they're automatically reconnected.

 Bluetooth devices are marked with the Bluetooth logo, shown in the margin. It's your assurance that the gizmo can work with other Bluetooth devices.

Activating Bluetooth on the Tab

To make the Bluetooth connection, first turn on the Tab's Bluetooth radio. Obey these directions:

1. **Open the Settings app and choose Connections.**

2. **Slide the master control by the Bluetooth item to the On position.**

When the master control is green, Bluetooth is activated.

When Bluetooth is on, the Bluetooth status icon appears, as shown in the margin.

To turn off Bluetooth, repeat the steps in this section: Slide the master control to the Off position.

TIP

From the And–Now–He–Tells–Us Department, you can quickly activate Bluetooth by using the Quick Settings on the notifications shade. Tap the Bluetooth icon to turn Bluetooth on or off.

Pairing with a Bluetooth device

To make the connection between your Galaxy Tab and a Bluetooth gizmo, follow these steps:

1. Ensure that Bluetooth is on.

Refer to the preceding section.

2. Turn on the Bluetooth gizmo.

3. On your Tab, open the Settings app and choose Connections.

4. Choose Bluetooth.

A list of available and paired devices is shown on the right side of the screen, similar to Figure 17-2. Don't fret if the device you want doesn't yet appear in the list.

5. If the other device has an option to become visible, select it.

For example, some Bluetooth gizmos have a tiny button to press that makes the device visible to other Bluetooth gizmos. (You don't need to make the Galaxy Tab visible for this operation.)

6. Select the device.

If the device doesn't show up, tap the SCAN button.

7. If necessary, type the device's passcode or otherwise acknowledge the connection.

For example, with a Bluetooth keyboard, you're prompted to type a series of numbers on the keyboard and then press the Enter or Return key. That action completes the pairing.

When the device is paired, you can begin using it.

Bluetooth switch

Actively look for devices.

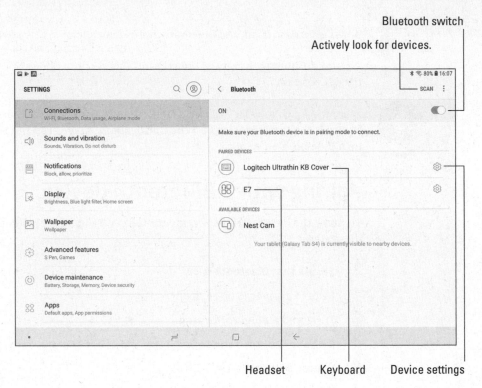

FIGURE 17-2:
Finding Bluetooth
gizmos.

Headset   Keyboard   Device settings

Connected devices appear in the Bluetooth Settings window, such as the Logitech keyboard cover, shown in Figure 17-2.

>> How you use the device depends on what it does. For example, a Bluetooth keyboard can be used for text input. You can use a Bluetooth speaker to listen to music played on the Tab.

>> It's rare to unpair a device. Should you need to, visit the Bluetooth screen (refer to Figure 17-2) and tap the Settings icon by the device's entry. Tap Unpair to break the Bluetooth connection and stop using the device.

>> Only unpair devices you don't plan to use again. Otherwise, turn off the Bluetooth device when you've finished using it.

REMEMBER

>> As wireless gizmos, Bluetooth peripherals consume lots of power. Don't forget to turn off the device, especially a battery-powered one, when you're no longer using it with your tablet.

IN THIS CHAPTER

» **Making the USB connection**

» **Using a USB cable to move files**

» **Sharing cloud storage**

» **Printing from your Tab**

» **Checking tablet storage**

» **Performing basic file management**

Chapter **18**

Connect, Share, and Store

Despite the device's wireless and mobile nature, you may desire to share information stored on your Galaxy Tab with other devices. Likewise, you might want to access from your tablet information stored elsewhere. Several methods are available to accomplish these tasks, although osmosis doesn't seem to be as effective as others. The most successful ways to connect and share are covered in this chapter, along with information on Galactic tablet storage.

The USB Connection

The most direct way to connect a Samsung Galaxy Tab to a computer is by using a wire — specifically, the wire nestled cozily in the heart of a USB cable.

Connecting the tablet to a computer

The USB connection between the Galaxy Tab and a computer works fastest when both devices are on and physically connected. That connection requires using the USB cable that comes with the tablet. Unlike the mythical Mobius cable, the Galaxy Tab's USB cable has two ends:

>> One end of the USB cable plugs into the computer.

>> The other end of the cable plugs into the bottom of the tablet.

The connectors are shaped differently and cannot be plugged in backward or upside down.

What happens after you connect your tablet to a computer is the topic of the next several sections.

REMEMBER

>> By connecting the tablet to a computer, you are adding, or *mounting,* its storage to the computer's storage system. The files and folders on the tablet can be accessed by using the computer's file management commands, which is how file transfer takes place.

>> Even if you don't use the USB cable to communicate with the computer, the tablet's battery charges when it's connected to a computer's USB port — as long as the computer is turned on, of course. Don't worry about a Slow Charging message; the fastest way to charge the Tab is by connecting it to a wall socket, not by using a computer's USB port.

Configuring the USB connection

A computer recognizes the Galaxy Tab's USB connection the instant you attach the device. To ensure that your Tab is configured for that type of connection, follow these directions:

1. **Connect the tablet to a computer.**

2. **If prompted to allow access to the tablet from the computer, tap the ALLOW button.**

   The tablet is mounted onto the PC's storage system. If not, or just to be certain, confirm the USB connection configuration.

3. **Choose the USB notification.**

The USB notification icon is shown in the margin. You may need to peruse the smaller items on the notification drawer to locate the USB notification.

4. **Ensure that the Transfer Files option is selected.**

Following these steps may fix the problem of a computer not recognizing the tablet.

REMEMBER

>> The USB notification appears when the tablet is connected to a computer. It's an ongoing notification that isn't dismissed until the connection is broken.

>> The Tab must be on and the touchscreen unlocked for the connection to be successful.

Dealing with the USB connection in Windows

Upon making the USB connection between the Galaxy Tab and a PC, a number of things happen. Don't let any of these things cause you undue alarm.

First, you may see some activity on the PC: drivers being installed and such. That's normal behavior any time you first connect a new USB gizmo to a Windows computer.

Second, you may see the AutoPlay notification, shown in Figure 18-1.

FIGURE 18-1:
Windows
AutoPlay
notification.

Third, choose an option from the AutoPlay notification, such as to open the one to open the device to view files. From that point on, you'll use Windows or a program on your computer to work with the files on your tablet. Later sections in this chapter provide the details.

Connecting your Tab to a Mac

Curiously enough, the Macintosh refuses to recognize the USB–Galaxy Tab connection. I wonder why?

To do the file transfer thing between your Mac and Galaxy tablet, you need to obtain the Android File Transfer app. Download that software from www.android.com/filetransfer.

Install the software. Run it. From that point on, when you connect your Galactic tablet to the Macintosh, you see a special window, similar to what's shown in Figure 18-2. It lists the tablet's folders and files. Use that window for file management, as covered later in this chapter.

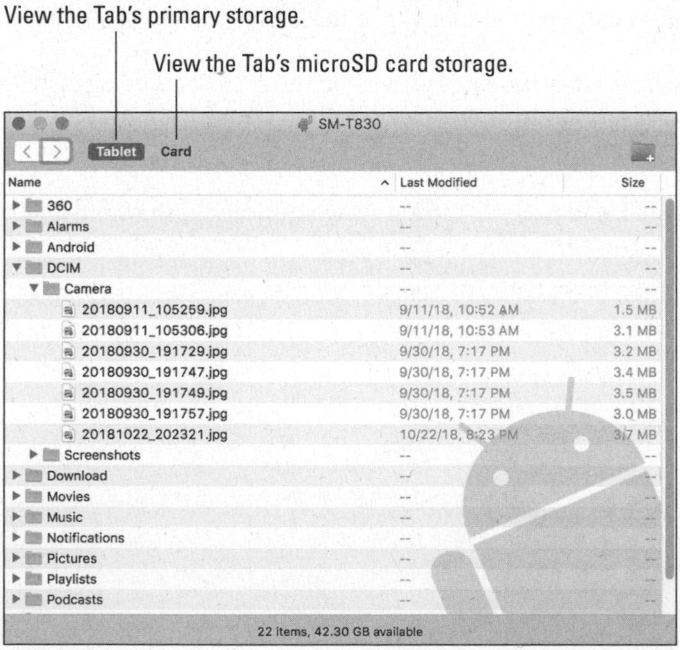

View the Tab's primary storage.

View the Tab's microSD card storage.

FIGURE 18-2: The Android File Transfer program.

Disconnecting the tablet from a computer

The process of disconnecting your tablet from a computer is cinchy: When you've finished transferring files, music, or other media, close all the programs and folders you've opened, specifically those you've used to work with the tablet's storage. Then you can disconnect the USB cable. That's it.

WARNING

It's a Bad Idea to unplug the tablet while you're transferring information or while a folder window is open on a PC. Doing so could damage the tablet's internal storage, rendering some of the information kept there unreadable. So just to be safe, before disconnecting, close those programs and folder windows you've opened.

Unlike other external storage on the Macintosh, there's no need to eject the tablet's storage when you've finished accessing it. Quit the Android File Transfer program on the Mac, and then unplug the tablet — or vice versa. The Mac won't get angry.

Files from Here, Files to There

The point of making the USB connection between your Galaxy Tab and a computer is to exchange files. You can't just wish the files over. Instead, I recommend following the advice in this section.

REMEMBER

A good understanding of basic file operations is necessary before you attempt file transfers between your computer and the Galaxy tablet. You need to know how to copy, move, rename, and delete files. It also helps to be familiar with what folders are and how they work. The good news is that you don't need to manually calculate a 64-bit cyclical redundancy check on the data, nor do you need to know what a parity bit is.

Transferring files by using the USB connection

I can think of plenty of reasons why you would want to copy a file from your computer to the tablet. You can transfer pictures and videos, music, or audio files or copy vCards exported from the computer's email program, which helps build the tablet's address book.

Follow these steps to copy files between a computer and the tablet:

1. **Connect the Galaxy Tab to the computer.**

   Specific directions are offered earlier in this chapter for both Windows and Mac OS X.

2. **On a PC, if the AutoPlay dialog box appears, select the Open Folder/ Device to View Files option.**

   When the AutoPlay dialog box doesn't appear, press the Win+E keyboard shortcut to open a File Explorer window. Choose This PC from the navigation drawer and locate your Galaxy Tab's storage icon(s) in that window.

   The tablet's folder window you see looks like any other folder in Windows. The difference is that the files and folders in that window are on the Galaxy Tab, not on the computer.

   On a Macintosh, the Android File Transfer program should start and appear on the screen. (Refer to Figure 18-2.)

3. **On the PC, open the folder that contains files you want to copy to the tablet, or into which you can to copy files from the tablet.**

   Open the folder that contains the files, or somehow have the file icons visible on the screen.

4. **Drag file icons between the two folders.**

   Figure 18-3 illustrates two folder windows that are open on a PC: one on the Galaxy Tab and the other on the PC. Use the mouse to drag icons between the two folders.

   The same file dragging technique can be used for transferring files from a Macintosh. Drag the icons to or from the Android File Transfer window, which works just like any folder window in the Finder.

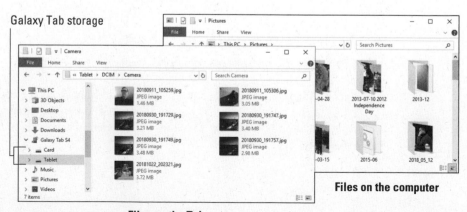

Galaxy Tab storage

Files on the computer

FIGURE 18-3:
Copying files to a
Galaxy tablet.

Files on the Tab

5. **Close the folder windows and disconnect the USB cable when you're done.**

Refer to specific instructions earlier in this chapter.

If you don't know where to copy files to your Tab, I offer these recommendations:

>> Copy music or audio files to the Music folder. Even then, a better way to copy music is to use a jukebox program on your computer to make the transfer. Refer to Chapter 14 for details.

>> Copy images to the Pictures folder. As with music, a better option is to use a photo management program to transfer images to the tablet in an organized fashion.

>> Copy all other files to the tablet's Download folder. After all, you're technically downloading files from the computer, so that seems like an obvious choice.

Sharing files in the cloud

A wireless way to share files between a computer and the Galaxy Tab is to use one of several online storage apps, such as Google Drive or Dropbox. These apps grant your tablet access to Internet file storage, also known as *cloud* storage. Any other device that uses the online storage also has access to the files. That makes Dropbox an ideal way to share and swap files.

The Tab comes with Google Drive. Dropbox is obtained, as well as other cloud storage apps, from the Play Store, as foretold in Chapter 16. Beyond installing those apps on your tablet, install their desktop counterparts on your computer or laptop. You get a modicum of free storage with your account, and you can pay to add more.

THE MEDIA CARD TRANSFER

Another way to get files between a computer and your Galactic tablet is to use the microSD card. It can be removed from the tablet and then inserted into a computer. From that point, the files on the card can be read by the computer just as they can be read from any media card.

See Chapter 1 for details on how to remove the microSD card from your tablet. You can't just yank out the thing! You also need a microSD adapter to insert the card into a media reader or USB port on the computer.

The files and folders accessed on cloud storage are available to both your computer and tablet. Copy, move, or create a file in one of the folders, and all your devices have access — provided an Internet connection is available.

> » File management on the Galaxy tablet is handled by the My Files app, in case you're into that sort of thing. See the later section "Managing files."

> » You can configure the tablet so that pictures and videos you take are instantly uploaded to your Google Drive or to Dropbox. See Chapter 13.

Sharing the screen

It's possible to view videos displayed or audio played on your Galaxy Tab S on an HDMI TV or monitor. As long as that TV or monitor has the Google Chromecast gizmo installed, screen sharing or *casting* is a snap. It's how I watch movies from Play Movies & TV, Netflix, and Hulu Plus on the big screen.

Here's a general idea of how casting works:

1. **Ensure that both the Tab and the casting gizmo access the same Wi-Fi network.**

2. **Open the app that has the media you want to play.**

   For example, open HBO Now to watch *Game of Thrones* or Spotify to listen to tunes.

3. **Ensure that the HDTV or monitor is on and the input with the Chromecast dongle is selected.**

   For example, on my Big, Expensive TV, Chromecast is on HDMI Input 1.

 4. **Tap the Chromecast icon.**

   The icon is shown in the margin. If it doesn't appear, redo Step 2.

   When multiple Chromecasts exist on the same Wi-Fi network, choose one from the list.

5. **Start playing the media.**

   The item you select appears on the HDTV or monitor.

Use the tablet to control the media: play, pause, and so on. With some apps, you may see additional details on the tablet, such as actor's names or other trivia.

To stop casting, tap the Chromecast icon again and choose DISCONNECT, or you can just turn off the TV or monitor.

Printing

You may not think of it as "file sharing," but using a printer with the Galaxy Tab is another way to get a file from here to there. It just happens that "there" is a printer, not a computer.

Printing on your Galaxy Tab works like this:

1. **View the material you want to print.**

You can print a web page or photo or any number of items.

2. **Tap the Action Overflow icon and choose the Print action.**

If the Print action isn't available, choose Share. On the list of sharing items, choose Print.

3. **Choose a printer from the Select Printer list or the action bar.**

Any printer available on the Wi-Fi network that the Tab is using shows up in the list.

To view printers from the action bar, tap the bar, as illustrated in Figure 18-4.

TIP

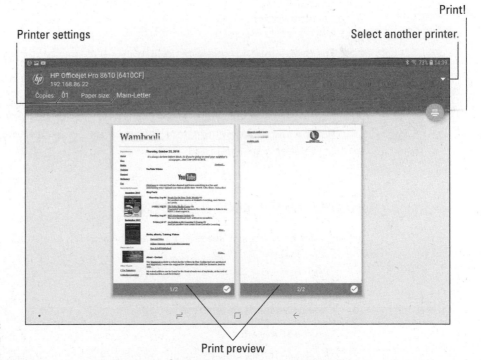

Print!

Printer settings   Select another printer.

Print preview

FIGURE 18-4: Choosing a printer.

4. **Change any print settings.**

For example, tap the Pages item to set the pages you want to print. Or change the number of copies. These are common print settings, similar to those you'd find in a computer's Print dialog box.

5. **Tap the big ol' Print button.**

The material you're viewing spews forth from the printer.

Not every app supports printing. The only way to know is to work through Steps 1 and 2. If you don't see the Print action, you can't print.

If the printer service for your printer isn't available, the Tab prompts you to download it. Proceed according to the directions presented on the screen.

Galactic Storage

Somewhere, deep in your Galaxy Tab's bosom, lies a storage device. It's like the hard drive in a computer. The thing can't be removed, but that's not the point. The point is that the storage is used for your apps, music, videos, pictures, and a host of other information.

>> The Galaxy Tab S4 comes with 64GB or 256GB of internal storage.

>> Removable storage is also available in the form of a microSD card.

TECHNICAL STUFF

>> A GB is a gigabyte, or 1 billion bytes (characters) of storage. A typical 2-hour movie consumes about 4GB of storage, but most things you store on the tablet — music and pictures, for example — take up only a sliver of storage. These slivers can and do add up over time.

Reviewing storage stats

To discover how storage space is used and how much is available on your tablet, follow these steps:

1. **Open the Settings app.**

2. **Choose Device Maintenance.**

3. **Tap the Storage icon.**

The screen details information about storage space in the tablet's internal storage, shown as Device Memory in Figure 18-5.

Total space

Free space   Used space   What's consuming storage

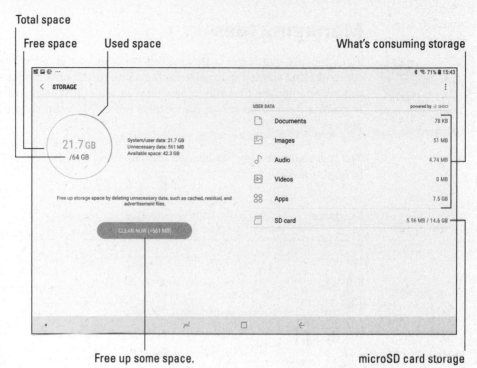

FIGURE 18-5:
Galaxy Tab
storage
information.

Free up some space.   microSD card storage

You can choose a category, such as Videos (refer to Figure 18-5) to see more details.

When a microSD card is installed, choose the SD Card item, shown in Figure 18-5. The details you see apply only to items stored on the microSD card.

TIP

TECHNICAL STUFF

>> Use the CLEAN NOW button to remove excess files and help improve the Tab's storage capacity.

>> Things that consume the most storage space are videos, music, and pictures, in that order.

>> Don't bemoan that the Total Space value is far less than the tablet's or media card's capacity. For example, in Figure 18-5, my 16GB media card shows only 14.83GB total space. The missing space is considered overhead, as are several gigabytes taken by the government for tax purposes.

Managing files

TECHNICAL STUFF

You probably didn't get a Galaxy Tab because you enjoy managing files on a computer and wanted to experience the same thrills on a mobile device. Even so, you can manipulate files and folders on your tablet just as you can on a computer. Is there a need to do so? Of course not! But if you want to get dirty with files, you can.

The tool that Samsung has blessed for managing files is the My Files app, shown in Figure 18-6.

Categories   Details

FIGURE 18-6:
The My Files app.

The My Files app is rather limited when compared with other file management apps. You can browse files, select them, delete, and share. Missing are other file management tools, such as an action to create a new folder.

Other file management apps are available at the Play Store. I prefer the Astro file management app, though others are available, and they all seem to do a keen job.

Chapter **19**

Apps and Widgets

A t last estimate, over 2.6 million apps are available at the Google Play Store. Why not collect them all?

Okay, perhaps not. But of the apps you do collect, you'll want to keep them neat and tidy. Organization is the key word, and organizing and managing your apps on the Galaxy Tab is a rather painless experience.

Apps and Widgets on the Home Screen

Lots of interesting doodads bespeckle your tablet's Home screen, like bugs on a windshield after a long trip. The two items you'll notice the most are apps and widgets.

Adding an app to the Home screen

When new apps are installed on the Galaxy Tab, a launcher icon is automatically affixed to the Home screen representing that app. You can perform this action manually, which helps put the apps you use most within easy reach. Here's how that works:

1. **Swipe the screen upward from the bottom.**

You see the Apps screen, home to all the apps on your tablet.

Some of the apps are held in folders.

2. **Long-press the app icon you want to add to the Home screen.**

After a moment, a list of actions pops up, similar to what's shown in Figure 19-1.

3. **Choose Add to Home.**

The app is placed on the Home screen.

FIGURE 19-1:
Stick an app on the Home screen.

For more precise action, after Step 3, drag the icon up to the top of the Apps screen, where you see the text Drag Here to Add to Home Screen, or you can continue to long-press the icon and eventually the Home screen appears. Continue to drag the icon to a specific location. Lift your finger to place it at that spot.

The app hasn't moved: What you see is a *launcher,* which is like a shortcut. You can still find the app on the Apps screen, but now the app is — more conveniently — available on the Home screen.

» Keep launchers on the Home screen for the apps you use most often.

» The later section "Moving icons and widgets" describes how to rearrange icons on the Home screen.

>> You can't stuff more icons on the Home screen than will fit in the grid, but the Tab gives you solutions for that crowded situation. One solution is to create an app folder; see the later section "Building app folders." A second solution is to add another Home screen page, which is covered in Chapter 20.

Slapping down widgets

Just as you can add apps to the Home screen, you can also add widgets. A *widget* works like a tiny, interactive or informative window, often providing a gateway into another app on the tablet.

To add a widget to the Home screen, follow these steps:

1. Swipe left or right to view a Home screen page large enough to accommodate the widget.

Unlike app launcher icons, widgets come in different sizes.

2. Long-press a blank part of the Home screen.

3. Tap the Widgets icon that appears at the bottom of the screen.

4. Swipe through the various pages of widgets to find the one you want.

TIP

Widgets are categorized by name. Some categories feature more than one widget; for example, the Calendar category features two. Somewhere on the widget's card you see its size relative to the standard launcher icon size. So a 2x2 widget is twice as wide and twice as tall as a launcher icon.

5. Long-press the widget you want to add.

6. Drag the widget to the Home screen.

Move the widget around to position it. As you drag the widget, existing launchers and widgets jiggle to make room.

7. Lift your finger.

8. Complete additional setup.

Some widgets require you to specify options. Complete the prompts as presented.

9. Resize the widget, if necessary.

If the widget grows an orange border, it can be resized. See the next section.

The variety of available widgets depends on the apps installed. Some apps come with widgets; some don't. Some widgets are independent of any app.

Fret not if you change your mind about the widget's location. See the later section "Moving icons and widgets," to obtain the proper *feng shui*.

Resizing a widget

Some widgets are resizable. You can change a widget's size right after plopping it down on the Home screen, or at any time, really: The secret is to long-press the widget. If it grows a blue box, as shown in Figure 19-2, you can change the widget's dimensions.

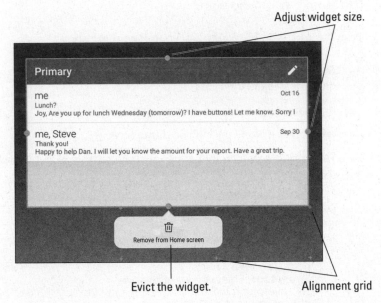

Adjust widget size.

Evict the widget.

Alignment grid

FIGURE 19-2: Adding a widget to the Home screen.

To resize, drag one of the dots in or out. Tap elsewhere on the touchscreen when you've finished resizing.

Moving icons and widgets

Icons and widgets are fastened to the Home screen by a digital version of the glue used on sticky notes; you can easily pick up an icon or a widget, move it around, and then re-stick it. Unlike sticky notes, the icons and widgets never just fall off, or so I'm told.

To move an icon or a widget, long-press it. Eventually, the item seems to lift and break free. Drag the item to another position on the Home screen. If you drag to the far left or far right, the icon or widget is sent to another Home screen page.

Removing an icon or a widget

To banish a launcher or widget from the Home screen, long-press it. A pop-up slate of icons appears, similar to what's shown in Figure 19-3.

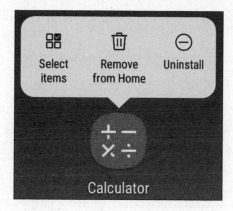

Choose the item Remove from Home, which is titled Remove from Home Screen for a widget. (Refer to Figure 19-2.) The launcher or widget is banished.

>> Removing an item from the Home screen does not delete the app or widget. See the later section "Uninstalling an app."

>> Long-pressing some launchers also displays a pop-up list of actions related to the app. For example, long-pressing the Clock launcher displays an action that lets you quickly set a timer.

>> If you change your mind, tap elsewhere on the Home screen to dismiss the pop-up bubble.

>> You can always add the launcher or widget back to the Home screen, as described elsewhere in this chapter.

TIP

REMEMBER

Building app folders

A great way to keep similar apps together on the Home screen is to bundle them into folders. For example, I have a Watch folder on my Tab full of apps that show movies and TV shows.

To create an app folder, follow these steps:

1. **Long-press an app launcher icon.**

A pop-up bubble appears, as shown in Figure 19-2.

2. **Choose Select Items.**

3. **Tap other launchers, those that you want to add to the folder.**

   You can swipe left or right to view different Home screens from which you can also select apps.

   ← If you change your mind at this point, tap the Back navigation icon to flee from the folder creation process.

4. **At the top of the screen, choose the Create Folder icon.**

   The folder appears, listing the apps you selected.

5. **Type a name for the folder.**

   Tap the Enter Folder Name field. Be short and descriptive, such as Social Networking, Music, or Samsung Stuff I Don't Use.

6. **Tap the Back navigation icon when you're done.**

Once a folder is created, you can add another launcher quickly by long-pressing its icon and dragging it into the folder.

To remove a launcher from a folder, tap to open and view the folder's contents. Long-press the icon and drag to the text at the top of the screen: Drag Here to Remove from Folder.

> » Folder icons are managed just like other icons on the Home screen. You can drag them around by long-pressing them, and you can delete them.

> » Change a folder's name by opening the folder and then tapping the folder's name. Use the onscreen keyboard to type a new folder name.

> » When the second-to-last icon is removed from a folder, the folder is also removed.

Manage Your Apps

The good news is that you really don't have to worry about managing apps on your Galaxy Tab. The Android operating system deftly handles that task for you. The bad news is that occasionally you may need to delicately dip your big toe into the app management sea. That's why I wrote this section.

Updating apps

 App updates happen all the time. They're automatic. Occasionally, you're called upon to perform a manual update. How can you tell? The Updates Available notification appears, looking similar to what's shown in the margin. Here's how to deal with that notification:

1. Open the Play Store app.

2. Tap the Side Menu icon to view the navigation drawer.

The Side Menu icon appears in the upper left corner of the screen (and in the margin). You may have to tap the Left Arrow icon (in the upper left corner of the screen) a few times before you can see the Side Menu icon.

3. Choose My Apps & Games.

4. Tap the Update All button.

5. If prompted, tap the Accept button to acknowledge an app's permission.

You may need to repeat this step for each app in need of an update.

The apps are individually updated. You can view the progress in the Play Store app or go off and do something else with your Tab.

>> Yes, the Tab must have an Internet connection to update apps. If the connection is broken, the apps update when the connection is reestablished.

>> Tap the STOP button on the My Apps screen to halt the updates.

Uninstalling an app

I can think of a few reasons to remove an app. It's with eager relish that I remove apps that don't work or somehow annoy me. It's also perfectly okay to remove redundant apps, such as when you have multiple eBook readers that you don't use. Whatever the reason, follow these directions to uninstall an app:

1. Start the Play Store app.

2. Tap the Side Menu icon to view the navigation drawer.

3. Choose My Apps & Games.

4. Tap the Installed tab.

5. Choose the app that offends you.

6. **Tap the Uninstall button.**

7. **Tap the OK button to confirm.**

The app is removed.

The app continues to appear on the All tab on the My Apps screen even after it's been removed. After all, you installed it once.

WARNING

>> You can always reinstall paid apps that you've uninstalled. You aren't charged twice for doing so.

>> You can't remove apps that are preinstalled on the tablet by either Samsung or your cellular provider. I'm sure there's probably a technical way to uninstall the apps, but seriously: Just don't use the apps if you want to remove them and discover that you can't.

TIP

>> You can also uninstall any app by long-pressing its launcher on the Home screen or its icon on the Apps screen: Choose the Uninstall option after long-pressing.

>> One way to avoid apps you don't like is to place them into an Apps screen folder. See the later section "Working with Apps screen folders."

Choosing a default app to open a file

Every so often, you may see the Open With or Complete Action Using prompt, similar to the one shown in Figure 19-4.

Open with

Docs   Word

JUST ONCE   ALWAYS

FIGURE 19-4: The Complete Action Using question is posed.

Multiple apps are available that can deal with your request. You pick one and then choose either ALWAYS or JUST ONCE.

When you choose ALWAYS, the same app is used for whatever action took place: compose email, listen to music, choose a photo, navigate, and so on.

When you choose JUST ONCE, you see the prompt again.

My advice is to choose JUST ONCE until you get sick of seeing the prompt. At that point, after choosing the same app over and over, choose ALWAYS.

The fear, of course, is that you'll make a mistake. Keep reading in the next section. Also see the later section "Setting a default app" for another type of default app. (The technology industry uses the word *default* way too often.)

Clearing a default app

Fret not, gentle reader. The settings chosen for the Complete Action Using prompt can be undone. For example, if you select the Docs app from Figure 19-4, you can undo that choice by following these steps:

1. **Open the Settings app.**

2. **Choose Apps.**

3. **Choose the app that opens as the default.**

   For example, from Figure 19-4, if you chose the Docs app, locate Docs in the list of apps and tap its entry.

4. **On the App Info screen, choose the item Set As Default.**

5. **Tap the CLEAR DEFAULTS button.**

After you clear the defaults for an app, you see the Open With or Complete Action Using prompt again. The next time you see it, however, make a better choice.

Setting a default app

Beyond apps that open files, the Galaxy Tab also has default apps for completing some system-wide tasks. For example, if you tap a web page link and the Tab has more than one web browser installed, you can choose which one to use.

To peruse default apps, heed these directions:

1. **Open the Settings app.**

2. **Choose the Apps category.**

3. **Tap the Action Overflow and choose Default Apps.**

The Action Overflow icon appears in the upper right corner of the screen and is shown in the margin.

If you desire to change one of the defaults, such as the Browser App, tap that item and select a new app from the list.

Beyond the Browser app, you can choose which app to run as the Home screen, and the Device Assistance app.

Shutting down an app run amok

It happens. Sometimes, an app goes crazy and just won't stop. Although Google tries to keep unstable apps out of the Play Store, not all technology is perfect. If you need to smite an errant app, follow these steps:

1. **Open the Settings app.**

2. **Choose the Apps category.**

3. **Tap the app's entry.**

4. **Tap the FORCE STOP button.**

If you see a warning, tap the OK button to stop the app.

WARNING

Only stop an app that you truly cannot halt in any other way.

If the app you want to halt appears as a launcher on the Home screen, long-press it to see a pop-up bubble appear. Choose the action Disable from the list.

TECHNICAL STUFF

The problem with randomly quitting an app is that data may get lost or damaged. At the worst, the tablet may become unstable. One way to fix that situation is to restart the device.

Organizing the Apps Screen

The go-to place for apps on your Galaxy Tab is the Apps screen. It lists all available apps on your tablet — plus, it's something you can customize to make accessing your apps easier.

Rearranging apps on the Apps screen

Apps appear on the Apps screen in any old order, with new ones you add showing up on the far right page. Two options are available to change their organization.

First, you can sort the apps. Heed these directions:

1. **On the Apps screen, tap the Action Overflow and choose Sort.**

2. **Choose Alphabetic Order.**

   The apps are rearranged from A to Z, with app folders appearing first on the far left page.

If you instead choose the Custom Order option, the apps appear as originally presented.

Second, you can drag app icons to change their order, though this operation is tricky: Long-press an app icon, and then slide it to a new position on the current page or to the far right to add a new Apps screen page. This operation can get you into trouble, as dragging the icon too far may set it on the Home screen, or you might unintentionally create an Apps Screen folder.

All changes made take effect immediately.

Working with Apps screen folders

Just as you can have an apps folder on the Home screen, the Apps screen can sport apps folders. These folders help organize apps on the Apps screen, which may help you locate certain types of apps.

The good news is that working with folders on the Apps screen works exactly like working with folders on the Home screen. Refer to the earlier section "Building app folders."

TIP

» I prefer to stick seldom-used apps into Apps screen folders. That way, they don't clutter the list when I'm looking for a specific app.

» Apps screen folders can be added to the Home screen just like any app. See the earlier section "Adding an app to the Home screen."

IN THIS CHAPTER

» **Changing the background image**

» **Adding Home screen pages**

» **Setting the screen lock timeout**

» **Customizing the Lock screen**

» **Changing the notification ringtone**

» **Adjusting the brightness**

Chapter **20**

Customize Your Tab

It's entirely possible to own the amazing Galaxy Tab for the rest of your life and never even once bother to customize the gizmo. It's not only possible, it's sad. That's because there exists great potential to make the tablet your own. You can alter so many things, from the way it looks to the way it sounds. The reason for customizing is not simply to change things because you can but to make the tablet work best for how you use it. After all, it's *your* Galaxy Tab.

Home Screen Settings

The Home screen is where the action happens on the Galaxy Tab. To help hone the Home page to meet your demands, several customization options are available. You can change the background image, but more importantly, you can add and remove Home screen pages.

Hanging new wallpaper

You can set wallpaper for the Home screen, Lock screen, or both. Your choices are any image you've taken or stored on the tablet or preset images supplied by Samsung's team of dedicated wallpaper artisans.

To set a new wallpaper for the Home screen, obey these steps:

1. **Long-press any empty part of the Home screen.**

   The empty part doesn't have a shortcut icon or widget floating on it.

2. **Tap the Wallpapers icon.**

3. **Select a wallpaper from the list, or choose From Gallery to choose an image stored on the Tab.**

   Swipe the list left or right to peruse your options. You'll see the preset wallpaper images supplied by Samsung, plus any photos you've used previously as wallpaper. On the far right you'll find the live wallpapers.

4. **Choose where to apply the wallpaper: Home screen, Lock screen, or Home and Lock screens.**

   You see a preview of how the wallpaper will appear. For larger or oddly proportioned images, you can adjust the preview to select which portion to use as wallpaper.

5. **Tap the Set Wallpaper button to confirm your choice.**

   The new wallpaper takes over the Home screen, Lock screen, or both.

Using the Tab to take images is covered in Chapter 12; editing images is covered in Chapter 13. Additional wallpapers are available online as well as from the Play Store; search for *Android wallpaper.*

Managing Home screen pages

How many pages can you find on the Home screen? I stopped tapping the Add icon after 12, so the maximum value is probably a lot!

To add another Home screen page on your Tab, follow these steps:

1. **Long-press a blank part of the Home screen.**

2. **Swipe the screen from right to left until you see the blank screen with the large plus sign on it.**

   Figure 20-1 shows what the Plus icon looks like. If you don't see it, you can't add more Home screen pages.

3. **Tap the Plus icon.**

   The new page appears, empty and ready for more icons and widgets.

4. **Tap the Back navigation icon to end Home screen editing.**

Add another Home screen page.

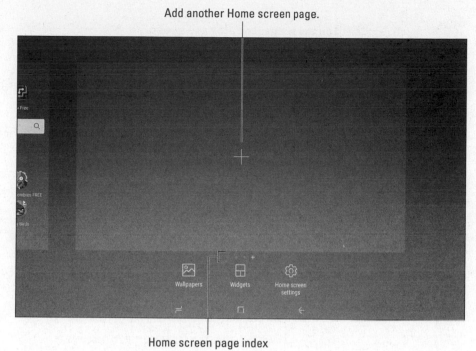

FIGURE 20-1:
Editing Home
screen pages.

Home screen page index

If you don't like the Home screen page's position, move a page: Edit the Home screen (refer to Step 1), and then long-press a page to drag it to a new position.

WARNING

>> To remove a Home screen page, tap the Delete icon in the upper right corner of the page. If the page has icons and widgets on it, you'll be asked to confirm.

>> There's no way to undo a Home screen panel deletion. You must add a new blank panel and then repopulate it with icons and widgets.

Setting the primary Home screen page

The wee Home icon on the page previews (refer to Figure 20-1) indicates the primary Home screen page. This page is summoned when you tap the Home navigation icon while viewing any Home screen page.

To set the primary Home screen page, follow these steps:

1. Long-press a blank part of the Home screen to edit the Home screen.

2. Swipe to the Home screen page you desire to make the primary Home screen page.

3. **Tap the Home icon atop the screen.**

   The icon is shown in the margin.

Adjusting the screen timeout

To manually lock your Galaxy Tab at any time, press the Power Lock key. That's why it's called the Power *Lock* key. When you don't manually lock the tablet, it automatically locks itself after a given period of inactivity.

The automatic-lock timeout value can be set from 15 seconds to several minutes. To set the timeout, obey these steps:

1. **Open the Settings app.**
2. **Choose Display.**
3. **On the right side of the screen, choose Screen Timeout.**
4. **Select a timeout value from the list.**

   I prefer 10 minutes. The standard value is 30 seconds.

The screen timeout measures inactivity; when you don't touch the screen or tap an icon or a button, the timer starts ticking. About 5 seconds before the timeout value you set (in Step 4), the touchscreen dims. Then it turns off, and the tablet locks. If you touch the screen before then, the timer is reset.

TECHNICAL
STUFF

The Lock screen has its own timeout. If you unlock the tablet but don't work the screen lock, the tablet locks itself automatically after about 10 seconds.

Lock Screen Configuration

The Lock screen is different from the Home screen, though the two locations share similar traits. As with the Home screen, you can customize the Lock screen. You can change the background, add app launcher shortcuts and info cards, and do all sorts of tricks.

For information on setting screen locks, refer to Chapter 21.

Adding Lock screen app shortcuts

You have the option of placing two app launcher icons on the Lock screen. You can use these Lock screen shortcuts to both unlock the tablet and immediately start the app: Swipe the app launcher icon on the Lock screen. If a secure screen lock is set, you must still work the lock to proceed.

As an example, to unlock the tablet and instantly use its camera, swipe the Camera app icon when you unlock your Tab.

To configure Lock screen shortcuts, heed these steps:

1. **Open the Settings app.**

2. **Choose Lock Screen.**

3. **On the right side of the screen, tap App Shortcuts.**

4. **Choose Left Shortcut and select an app from the list displayed.**

5. **Choose Right Shortcut and select an app.**

To disable a shortcut, tap the On master control (atop the screen in Steps 4 and 5).

Displaying FaceWidgets

A *FaceWidget* is a handy card that displays useful information on the Tab's Lock screen. It's like a Home screen widget, but its contents are visible when you press the Power Lock key and before you unlock the touchscreen.

To add a FaceWidget to the lock screen, follow these steps:

1. **Open the Settings app.**

2. **Choose Lock Screen.**

3. **Choose FaceWidgets from the list of items on the right side of the screen.**

4. **Activate the master control by the FaceWidget you want to add to the Lock screen.**

The FaceWidgets appear in the same location as the time display on the Lock screen. To peruse the FaceWidgets, swipe the time left or right. Continue swiping to cycle through all available FaceWidgets.

Various Galactic Adjustments

You have plenty of things to adjust, tune, and tweak on your Galaxy Tab. The Settings app is the gateway to all these options, and I'm sure you could waste hours there if you had hours to waste. My guess is that your time is precious; therefore, this section highlights some of the more worthy options and settings.

Singing a different tune

The Sounds and Vibration screen is where you control which sound the tablet plays as a ringtone, but it's also where you can set volume and vibration options. To view this screen, open the Settings app and choose the Sounds and Vibration category.

Here are the worthy options to set as found on the Sound and Vibration screen:

Notification Sounds: Choose which sound you want to hear for a notification alert, or choose the Silent option to mute all notification sounds.

Touch Sounds: Set this item to On if you prefer that the tablet provide audible feedback when you tap the screen.

Keyboard sound and vibration: Set these two items to provide audio and haptic feedback when using the onscreen keyboard.

Vibration Feedback: Use this item to activate tablet vibration.

TIP

>> Sound options are set by using the Tab's internal media controls. You can, however, install a special media app to set sounds for your device. If so, you'll be prompted to use that app when you choose notification and other sounds.

>> Individual apps often sport their own notification sounds. For example, Facebook and Twitter set their sounds by using the Settings action in those individual apps.

Changing visual settings

Probably the key thing you want to adjust visually on your Galaxy Tab is the screen's brightness. To set how bright or dim the touchscreen appears, follow these steps:

1. **Open the Settings app.**

2. **Choose Display.**

3. **Adjust the brightness slider.**

   Left is dim; right is bright.

Activate the master control by the Auto Brightness item to direct the Tab to automatically adjust its brightness based on the ambient light.

To make the Tab easier to see at night, activate the master control by the Blue Light Filter item, also found on the Display screen in the Settings app. Having this feature active removes some of the blue spectrum from the display, making it easier to see at night as well as easier for you to make the transition to sleep.

A Quick Settings shortcut for the Blue Light Filter is also available. It's icon is shown in the margin.

TIP

>> A shortcut to setting the brightness can be found in the notifications shade, just below the Quick Settings.

>> The screen timeout is also considered a visual setting. Refer to the earlier section "Adjusting the screen timeout."

>> See Chapter 3 for more information on Quick Settings.

Chapter **21**

Galactic Security

As a citizen of the 21st century, you no doubt have an extensive digital presence. Your footprint includes accounts, passwords — perhaps even financial information — and you tote around access to that information, if not the information itself, with your Galaxy Tab everywhere you go. Obviously, security is an issue. Don't take it too lightly.

Lock Your Tablet

If you keep anything important on your Galaxy Tab, or when you have multiple users on the same tablet or a corporate email account, you need Lock screen security. This security must be more than the simple Swipe screen lock.

Finding the screen locks

Lock screen security is set from the Screen Lock Type screen. Here's how to get there:

1. **Open the Settings app.**

2. **Choose Lock Screen.**

3. On the right side of the screen, choose Screen Lock Type.

4. Work any existing screen lock to continue.

When the Swipe or None lock is set, you just see the Screen Lock Type screen.

Several locks are available on the Select Screen Lock screen. They are:

>> **Swipe:** Unlock the tablet by swiping your finger across the screen.

>> **Pattern:** Trace a pattern on the touchscreen to unlock the tablet.

>> **PIN:** Unlock the tablet by typing a personal identification number (PIN).

>> **Password:** Type a password to unlock the tablet.

>> **None:** The screen doesn't lock.

Biometric locks are also available, including face scan, iris scan, and facial recognition.

The most secure locks are PIN and Password. The Pattern lock and biometrics come in second, but they require a PIN or a password as backup. The Swipe and None locks are nonsecure.

Removing the screen lock

You use the Screen Lock Type screen to not only place a lock on the tablet but also remove locks.

After visiting the Screen Lock window, as described in the preceding section, you can choose the None option to remove all screen locks. To restore the original screen lock, choose Swipe.

Setting a PIN

Perhaps the most common, and the second most secure method, of locking the tablet is to use a PIN, or *personal identification number*. This type of screen lock is also employed as a backup for less-secure screen unlocking methods.

A *PIN lock* is a code between 4 and 16 numbers long. It contains only numbers, 0 through 9. To set a PIN lock, follow the directions in the earlier section "Finding the screen locks" to reach the Screen Lock Type screen. Choose PIN from the list of locks.

Use the onscreen keypad to type your PIN once, and tap the Continue button. Type the PIN again to confirm that you know it. Tap OK. The next time you turn on or unlock the tablet, you must type the PIN to get access.

To disable the PIN, reset the security level as described in the preceding section.

WARNING

I know of no recovery method available should you forget your tablet's PIN. Don't forget it!

Assigning a password

The most secure — and therefore the most arduous — screen lock is a full-on password. Unlike a PIN (refer to the preceding section), a *password* can contain numbers, symbols, and both uppercase and lowercase letters.

Set a password by choosing Password from the Screen Lock Type screen; refer to the earlier section "Finding the screen locks" for information on getting to that screen. The password you select must be at least four characters long. Longer passwords are more secure.

You're prompted to type the password whenever you unlock the tablet or when you try to change the screen lock. Tap the OK button to accept the password you've typed.

WARNING

You're out of luck if you forget the Tab's password.

Creating an unlock pattern

One of the most common ways to lock a Galaxy Tab is to apply an *unlock pattern:* The pattern must be traced exactly as it was created to unlock the device and gain access to your apps and other tablet features.

1. **Summon the Screen Lock window.**

Refer to the earlier section "Finding the screen locks."

2. **Choose Pattern.**

If you've not yet set a pattern lock, you may see a tutorial describing the process; tap the Next button to skip over the dreary directions.

3. **Trace an unlock pattern.**

Use Figure 21-1 as your inspiration. You can trace over the dots in any order, but you can trace over a dot only once. The pattern must cover at least four dots.

4. **Tap the CONTINUE button.**

5. **Redraw the pattern.**

You need to prove to the doubtful tablet that you know the pattern.

6. **Tap the CONFIRM button.**

And the pattern lock is set.

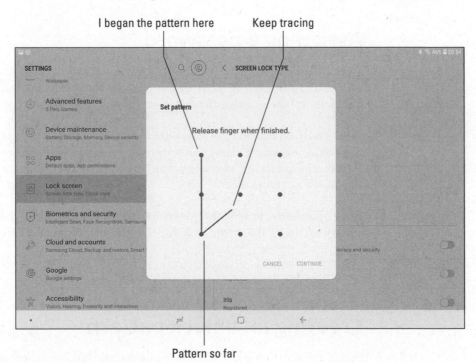

FIGURE 21-1:
Setting an
unlock pattern.

I began the pattern here   Keep tracing

Pattern so far

TIP

To ensure that the pattern shows up, from the Lock Screen category choose Secure Lock Settings. Trace the pattern. On the Secure Lock Settings screen, ensure that the option Make Pattern Visible is active. For even more security, you can deselect the option, but you must be sure to remember how — and where — the pattern goes.

Unlocking the tablet with your face

You can use various facial features to provide a biometric lock for your Tab. Providing that you have a face, try out some of these options:

Face: Use facial recognition to unlock the tablet.

Iris: Use your iris patterns to unlock the Tab.

Intelligent Scan: Use both Face and Iris options to unlock the Tab.

To set up these screen locks, you must first register your face. Choose one of the options from the Screen Lock Type screen and follow the onscreen directions. I strongly recommend that you hold the tablet as you will use it; don't hold it out in front of you like you're taking a selfie unless that's how you always work with the tablet. For example, if you keep the Tab in your lap, register your biometrics while the device is in your lap.

Biometric locks can be fun, but they are not secure. Also, their performance is iffy, because many factors affect facial recognition. I consider this feature to be more of a toy than anything practical.

Other Tab Security

Locking your tablet with a secure screen lock works wonders as far as keeping your tablet's information safe. The screen lock doesn't help, however, should your tablet get lost or stolen. That's when more tools are required for a swift recovery.

Adding owner info text

If your Galaxy Tab someday gets lost, it would be nice if a good Samaritan found it. What would be even more helpful is if you had some information on the Lock screen to help that kind person find you and return your Tab.

Follow these steps to add owner information text to the Lock screen:

1. Visit the Settings app.

2. Choose Lock Screen from the categories on the left side of the screen.

3. On the right side of the screen, choose Contact Information.

4. Type text in the box.

You can type more than one line of text, though the information is displayed on the Lock screen as a single line.

TIP

5. Tap the DONE button.

Whatever text you type in the box appears on the Lock screen. Therefore, I recommend typing something useful, as the command suggests: your name, phone number, and email address, for example. This way, should you lose your tablet and an honest person finds it, that person can get it back to you.

Hiding Lock screen notifications

The Tab's Lock screen shows a clutch of notifications, which appear as individual items that can be expanded to view more details. Sometimes those details, such as bank account information or perhaps an email from your ex's attorney, are better left off the Lock screen. If you agree, obey these steps:

1. **Open the Settings app.**

2. **Choose Lock Screen.**

3. **Choose Notifications.**

   The Notifications screen opens for showing or hiding Lock screen notification options.

Here are your options:

>> To remove all Lock screen notifications, slide the master control to the Off position.

>> To see the notification type but not any details, activate the master control by the Hide Content item.

>> For the most limited presentation, activate the master control by the option Notification Icons Only.

Use the preview window on the Notifications screen to see how potential Lock screen notifications present themselves.

Find your lost tablet

Someday, you may lose your beloved Galaxy Tab. It might be for a few panic-filled seconds, or it could be for forever. The hardware solution is to weld a heavy object to the tablet, such as an anvil or a rhinoceros, but that strategy kind of defeats the entire mobile/wireless paradigm. (Well, not so much the rhino.) The software solution is the better option.

For your Google account, follow these steps:

1. **On a computer or another mobile device, visit** google.com/android/find.

   Your Galaxy Tab is missing, remember? You must use another device to find it.

2. **On the Find My Device web page, choose your Android gizmo.**

   If you have multiple gizmos, each is listed atop the window. Choose the Galaxy Tab.

3. **Select an option to deal with the lost gizmo.**

   Your choices are described in this list:

   Play Sound: The Tab rings for 5 minutes as you frantically hunt for it.

   Secure Device: The Tab is remotely locked. You can select a message to display on the device.

   Erase Device: All your personal information is erased from the Tab. After performing this operation, you will no longer be able to locate the device.

In addition to the options available on the page, you see a map page that lists an approximate location for the Tab. You can use that to find the device, should you have left it nearby or perchance at the local apothecary or brothel.

On your Tab, in the Settings app's Biometrics and Security category, is an option titled Find My Mobile. This feature also works to locate a missing tablet, providing you have a Samsung account and have configured the service. Google's Find My Device service requires neither additional configuration nor the creation of a new account, which is why I prefer it.

Avoiding Android viruses

I am often asked about antivirus security software for the Galaxy Tab. The requests probably come from the PC world, where viruses are real and deadly and all too frequent. Fortunately, such isn't the case on the Tab.

Evil and malicious apps do exist, but they don't advertise themselves as such. The key to knowing whether an app is evil is to look at its permissions. For example, if a simple grocery list app accesses the tablet's address book and the app doesn't need to do so, it's suspect.

If you're truly concerned about an Android virus, you can activate Device Security. Heed these directions:

1. **Open the Settings app.**

2. **Choose Device Maintenance.**

3. **Tap the icon labeled Device Security.**

4. **Tap the ACTIVATE button.**

5. **Tap the AGREE button to accept the terms.**

   Device security is activated.

To proceed with a virus scan, tap the SCAN TABLET button. Any questionable items are flagged on the screen.

>> As far as I can tell, the Tab's Device Security feature isn't subscription-based. Some of the other options on that screen might be.

>> In the history of the Android operating system, only a handful of malicious apps have been distributed, and most of them were found in Asia. Google routinely removes these apps from the Play Store, and a feature of the Android operating system even lets Google remove apps from your phone. So, you're pretty safe.

>> Generally speaking, avoid "hacker" apps, porn, and those apps that use social engineering to make you do things on your Galaxy Tab that you wouldn't otherwise do, such as remove the screen lock or volunteer personal information.

TIP

Performing a factory data reset

The most secure thing you can do with your information on the Galaxy Tab is to erase it all. The procedure is known as a *factory data reset.* It effectively restores the Tab back to its original state, as you received the device after opening the box, though with all Android updates and security patches still in place.

A factory data reset is a drastic thing. It not only removes all information from storage but also erases all your accounts. Don't take this step lightly!

WARNING

When you're ready to erase all the tablet's data, follow these steps:

1. **Start the Settings app.**

2. **Choose General Management.**

3. **Choose Factory Data Reset.**

4. **On the right side of the screen, choose Reset.**

5. **Choose Factory Data Reset.**

6. **Tap the RESET button.**

7. **If prompted, work the screen lock.**

   This level of security prevents others from idly messing with your Tab.

8. **Tap the DELETE ALL button to confirm.**

   All the information you've set or stored on the tablet is purged, including all your accounts, any apps you've downloaded, music — everything.

TIP

Practical instances when a factory data reset is necessary include selling your tablet, giving it to someone else to use, or retiring it when you get a new one. These are the perfect times to perform a factory data reset.

It's Everyone's Tab!

Computers have long had the capability to allow multiple users on the same device. Each person has his own account and customized items in his account. It's a good idea for a computer, but for a tablet?

Your Galaxy Tab can handle several users. Though I would suggest that each person get his own Tab (and his own copy of this book), that's not always practical. A better solution is to give all the folks, including the kiddies, their own user accounts on the device.

Adding another user

When someone else desires to use your Galaxy Tab, don't just hand it over! Instead, create a custom user account for that person.

First, apply a screen lock to your account on the Tab. See the earlier section "Lock Your Tablet." Ensure that the screen lock has at least medium-level security; PIN or Password locks are preferred.

Second, get together with the other human and follow these steps:

1. **Open the Settings app.**

2. **Choose Cloud and Accounts from the left side of the screen.**

3. **Choose Users from the list of items on the right side of the screen.**

4. **Choose Add User or Profile.**

5. **Choose User.**

   See the later section "Configuring the Tab for a kid's account" for information on the Restricted Profile account type.

6. **Tap the OK button after ignoring the Add User info.**

7. **Tap the SET UP NOW button, and then hand the Tab over to the other person.**

   The other person can continue configuring the device just as you did when you first set up the Tab.

Setting up an account includes specifying a Google/Gmail account and setting other options. Once this task is completed, the other user can use the Tab under his own account. All settings, apps, email, and other items are unique to his account. And he cannot access your account unless he knows how to work your screen lock.

» I recommend that each user on the Tab have an account protected with a medium- to high-security screen lock.

» The tablet's first user (most likely you) is the main user, the one who has primary administrative control.

» Remove an account by following Steps 1 through 3 in this section. Tap the Delete (trash can) icon on the account you want to remove. Tap the DELETE button to confirm.

Switching users

Multiple accounts on the Galaxy Tab appear in the upper right corner of the Lock screen. The current account is shown as a bubble. To select another account, tap the bubble, as illustrated in Figure 21-2. Choose the account from the list, and then work the Lock screen to gain access.

REMEMBER

When you've finished using the tablet, lock the screen. Other users can then access their own accounts as described in this section.

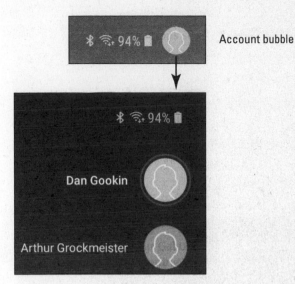

Account bubble

FIGURE 21-2:
Choosing an
account on the
Lock screen.

Configuring the Tab for a kid's account

Don't just hand over your Galaxy Tab to Peanut! Craft a kid's account for him to use. That way, you can set which apps are allowed or denied, as well as prevent him from downloading millions of dollars of apps, music, and video.

To add a kid's account, follow the steps in the earlier section "Adding another user." Choose the Restricted Profile account type. Yes, you need to apply a secure screen lock to your own account before you add the kid's account.

After creating the account, you see the Application/Content Restrictions screen. Here's what to do next:

1. **Tap the account name, New Restricted Account, to replace it with your child's name — or whatever name he chooses.**

2. **Place a check mark by the Location Access item if you want his location tracked as he uses the tablet.**

   Most parents prefer to keep this item unchecked.

3. **Swipe through the list of programs and place a check mark by the ones you would allow your wee one to use.**

   These would include various games or whatever other apps you deem appropriate. Some apps, such as Google, Netflix, and Play Movies & TV, feature a Settings icon. Tap this icon to make further adjustments, such as determining what level of entertainment would be appropriate for your child.

See the preceding section for information on switching to the kid's account.

Chapter **22**

Taking the Tab with You

Last time I checked, the Galaxy Tab didn't have a rolling tread, like a tank. That would be nifty, and I'm sure that more Real Men would buy a Tab with a tank tread, but that's not my point: Your tablet is a mobile device. It's wireless. It runs on battery power. You can take the Galaxy Tab with you everywhere you go and not get those peculiar looks you get when you take the washing machine with you.

How far can you go with your Tab? As far as you want. As long as you can carry the tablet with you, it goes where you go. How it functions may change, depending on your environment.

Before You Go

Unless the house is on fire, you should prepare several items before leaving on a trip with your Galactic tablet. First and most important, of course, is to charge the thing. I plug my tablet in overnight before leaving the next day.

Consider getting movies, eBooks, and music for the road. I prefer to sit and stew over the Play Books online library before I leave, as opposed to wandering aimlessly in some airport sundry store, trying hard to focus on the good books rather than on the salty snacks. Chapter 15 covers reading eBooks on your Galaxy Tab.

Also — and this is important: Remember to download movies, eBooks, and music, especially if you'll be somewhere that the Internet is unavailable. Chapter 16 offers information on keeping these items on your Tab.

Another nifty thing to do is to save some web pages for later reading. I usually start my day by perusing online articles and angry letters to the editor in my local paper. Because I don't have time to read that stuff before I leave (and because I do have time on the plane and I'm extremely unwilling to pay for in-flight Wi-Fi), I save my favorite websites for later reading. Here's how to save a web page by using the Internet app:

1. **Navigate to the page you want to save for later reading.**

2. **Tap the Download icon in the address bar to save the page.**

   The icon is shown in the margin.

Repeat these steps for each web page you want to read when offline.

To view the page, tap the Action Overflow icon and choose Downloads. Choose a saved web page from the list to view offline.

Also consider loading up your Tab with plenty of games. Sure, you can convince yourself that you really, really are going to get some work done during your flight. You may have even promised the boss, but games really do help make the time pass quickly.

Finally, don't forget your tickets! Nearly every airline offers apps that make traveling easy because they generate notifications for your schedule and provide timely gate changes or flight delays. Plus, you can use the Tab as your electronic boarding pass. Search the Play Store to see whether your preferred airline offers an app.

Galaxy Tab Travel Tips

I'm not a frequent flier, but I am a nerd. The most amount of junk I've carried with me on a flight is two laptop computers and three smartphones. I know that's not a record, but it's enough to warrant my list of travel tips, all of which apply to taking the Galaxy Tab with you on an extended journey:

> » Bring the tablet's AC adapter and USB cable with you. Put them in your carry-on luggage. Many airports feature USB chargers, so you can charge the tablet in an airport if you need to.

>> At the security checkpoint, place the tablet in a bin by itself or with other electronics. If you're TSA-Pre (checked through security ahead of time), you don't have to put the Tab in its own bin, but check with the TSA agents to confirm.

>> Scan for the airport's Wi-Fi service. Most airports don't charge for the service, although you may have to agree to terms by using the tablet's web browser app to visit the airport's website.

Into the Wild Blue Yonder

It truly is the most trendy of things to be aloft with the latest mobile gizmo. As with taking a smartphone on a plane, however, you must follow some rules.

The good news is that because your Galaxy Tab isn't a smartphone, you can leave it on for the duration of the flight. All you need to do is place the tablet into Airplane mode. Follow these steps just before takeoff:

1. **Open the Settings app.**

2. **Choose Connections.**

3. **Slide the master control by the Airplane Mode item to the On position.**

   The tablet turns off its Wi-Fi and Bluetooth radios.

While the tablet is in Airplane mode, a special icon appears in the status area at the top of the screen.

TIP

And now, for the shortcut: Pull down the notifications shade and touch the Airplane Mode Quick Setting.

By the way, you can reactivate Wi-Fi and Bluetooth while the tablet is in Airplane mode. It's okay to do so, especially when in-flight Wi-Fi is available or you use Bluetooth headphones.

To exit Airplane mode, repeat the steps in this section to deactivate it.

>> When inflight Wi-Fi isn't available, consider downloading eBooks, music, and web pages to your Tab. Refer to the section "Before You Go," earlier in this chapter.

» You can still compose email while the tablet is in Airplane mode. The messages aren't sent until an Internet connection is again established.

» Airplane mode disables the tablet's Bluetooth radio and GPS. If you have an LTE Tab, its mobile data radio is also disabled.

The Galaxy Goes Abroad

Have no worries taking your Galaxy Tab abroad. The Wi-Fi Tab most definitely can use any Wi-Fi Internet access available. The LTE Tab might be able to use the mobile data network at your location, though you should take some precautions. After all, you don't want to incur data roaming charges, especially when they're priced in *zloty* or *pengö*.

Traveling overseas with the tablet

The Galaxy Tab works great overseas. The two resources you need are a way to recharge the battery and a way to access Wi-Fi. As long as you have both of them, you're pretty much set. (Data roaming is covered in the next section.)

The tablet's AC plug can easily plug into a foreign wall socket, which allows you to charge the tablet in outer Wamboolistan. I charged my tablet nightly while I spent time in France, and it worked like a charm. All you need is an adapter. You don't need a transformer or a power converter, just the dongle that allows you to plug into a wall socket. That's it. You're good.

Wi-Fi is universal, and as long as your location offers this service, you can connect the tablet and pick up your email, browse the web, or do whatever other Internet activities you desire. Even if you have to pay for Wi-Fi access, I believe that you'll find it less expensive than paying a data roaming charge.

TIP

» If you want to use Skype for placing an overseas phone call, you need to set up Skype credit. See Chapter 8 for more information on making Skype calls.

» Many overseas hotels and B&Bs offer free Wi-Fi. When your hotel doesn't, visit an Internet café. These locations are far more numerous in countries outside the US, and the access is reasonably priced.

Disabling mobile data and data roaming

When I've taken my cellular Galaxy Tab abroad, I've kept it in Airplane mode. If you do that, there's no chance of incurring data roaming charges. Instead, use the tablet's Wi-Fi for Internet access.

Just to be sure that your Tab doesn't latch on to a foreign cellular service and, say, download 80 gigabytes of app updates (not that my Tab has ever done such a thing), consider disabling mobile data. Heed these steps:

1. **Open the Settings app.**

2. **Choose Connections.**

3. **Choose Mobile Network or Cellular Network on the right side of the screen.**

4. **Ensure that the Data Roaming item is disabled.**

    And you're good to go — literally.

Of course, you don't need to disable mobile data or keep the tablet stuck in Airplane mode. You can just wait for your data bill's arrival in the mail. I prefer not to have such a surprise.

TIP

>> Before you travel abroad, contact your cellular provider and ask about overseas data roaming. A subscription service or other options may be available, especially when you plan to stay overseas for an extended length of time.

>> If you do get an overseas subscription, repeat the steps in this section and most definitely disable Data Roaming. You don't want the tablet to be roaming overseas.

REMEMBER

>> With the tablet's mobile data disabled, you must rely entirely upon Wi-Fi for Internet access. See Chapter 17.

Chapter **23**

Maintenance and Troubleshooting

I hear that the maintenance on the Eiffel Tower is arduous. Once a year, the French utterly disassemble the landmark; individually scrub every girder, nut, and bolt; and then put it all back together. The entire operation is performed early in the morning, so that when Paris wakes up, no one notices. Well, people notice that the Tower is cleaner, but no one is aware that it was completely disassembled, cleaned, and rebuilt. Truly, the French are amazing.

Fortunately, maintenance for your Galaxy Tab isn't as consuming as maintenance on one of the world's great monuments. For example, cleaning the tablet takes mere seconds, and no disassembly is required. It's cinchy! Beyond covering maintenance, this chapter offers suggestions for using the battery — plus, it gives you some helpful tips and Q&A.

Regular Galactic Maintenance

Relax. Maintenance for your Galaxy Tab is simple and quick. Basically, I can summarize it in three words: Keep it clean. Beyond that, another task worthy of attention is backing up the information stored on your tablet.

Keeping it clean

You probably already keep your tablet clean. Perhaps you're one of those people who use their sleeves to wipe the touchscreen. Of course, better than your sleeve is something called a *microfiber cloth*. This item can be found at any computer- or office-supply store.

WARNING

>> Never clean the touchscreen by using a liquid — especially ammonia or alcohol. Those substances damage the touchscreen, rendering it unable to read your input. Further, such harsh chemicals can smudge the display, making it more difficult to see.

>> If the screen keeps getting dirty, consider adding a screen protector. This specially designed cover prevents the screen from getting scratched or dirty while also letting you use your finger on the touchscreen. Be sure that the screen protector is designed for use with your Samsung Galaxy Tab model.

Backing up your stuff

A *backup* is a safety copy of information. For your tablet, the backup copy includes contact information, music, photos, video, and apps, plus any settings you've made to customize your tablet. The good news is that all this information is backed up to your Google account automatically. To confirm that your Google account information is being backed up, heed these steps:

1. **Open the Settings app.**

2. **Choose Cloud and Accounts.**

3. **On the right side of the screen, choose Backup and Restore.**

4. **Ensure that check marks appear by the item Back Up My Data.**

Any other data you want to save from your tablet can be synchronized over cloud storage. For example, documents you obtain can be copied to cloud storage so that they're available on your other devices. This topic is covered in Chapter 18.

Updating the system

Updates for your Galaxy Tab come in three flavors: security, Samsung, and Google.

Security patches arrive monthly. These updates prevent the bad guys from using known exploits to gain control over your device.

Samsung updates arrive whenever Samsung deems an update necessary. These include hardware and security updates not covered by the routine security patches.

Google occasionally updates the Android operating system, though such an update is more likely to come from Samsung than from Google.

When an update is available, a notification alerts you. My advice is to choose the update and install it at once or schedule it for a convenient time. Updates are important! Don't skip them.

TIP

If possible, connect the tablet to a power source during a software update. You don't want the battery to die in the middle of the operation.

Battery Care and Feeding

Perhaps the most important item you can monitor and maintain on your Galaxy Tab is its battery. The battery supplies the necessary electrical juice by which the device operates. Without battery power, your tablet is basically an expensive trivet. Keep an eye on the battery.

Monitoring the battery

You can find information about the Galaxy tablet's battery status in the upper right corner of the screen, next to the current time in the status area. The icons used to display battery status are shown in Figure 23-1.

You might also see an icon for a dead battery, but for some reason I can't get my tablet to turn on and display that icon.

REMEMBER

Heed those low-battery warnings! The Galaxy Tab alerts you when the battery level gets low, at about 15 percent capacity.

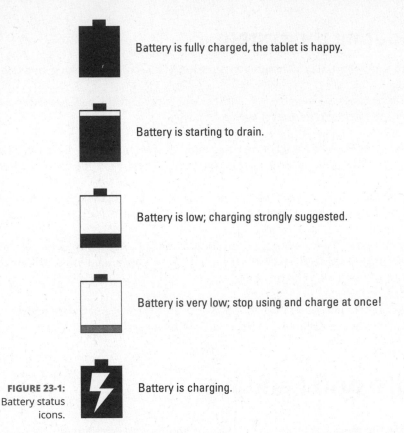

Battery is fully charged, the tablet is happy.

Battery is starting to drain.

Battery is low; charging strongly suggested.

Battery is very low; stop using and charge at once!

FIGURE 23-1:
Battery status
icons.

Battery is charging.

Another warning shows up when the battery level gets seriously low, below 5 percent — but why wait for that? Take action at the 15 percent warning.

>> When the battery level is too low, the tablet shuts itself off.

TIP

>> The best way to deal with low battery power is to connect the tablet to a power source: Either plug it into a wall socket or connect it to a computer by using a USB cable. The tablet begins charging itself immediately; plus, you can use the device while it's charging.

>> You don't have to fully charge the tablet to use it. When you have only 20 minutes to charge and you get only a 70 percent battery level, that's great. Well, it's not great, but it's far better than a lower battery level.

TECHNICAL STUFF

>> Battery percentage values are best-guess estimates. The typical Galaxy Tab has a hearty battery that can last for hours. But when the battery meter gets low, the battery drains faster. So, if you get 8 hours of use from the tablet and the battery meter shows 20 percent left, those numbers don't imply that 20 percent equals 2 more hours of use. In practice, the amount of time you have left is much less than that. As a rule, when the battery percentage value gets low, the battery appears to drain faster.

Determining what is sucking up power

The Galaxy tablet is smart enough to know which of its features use the most battery power. To check it out for yourself, follow these steps:

1. **Open the Settings app.**

2. **Choose Device Maintenance.**

3. **Tap the Battery icon.**

    You see the Battery screen, similar to the one shown in Figure 23-2.

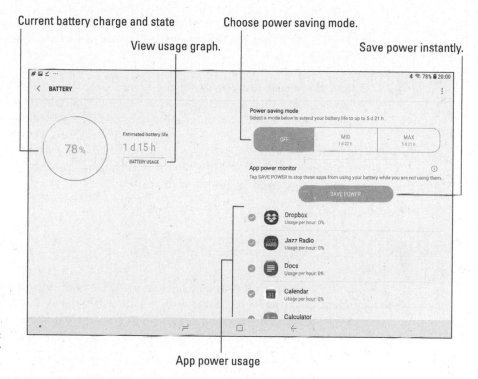

Current battery charge and state

View usage graph.

Choose power saving mode.

Save power instantly.

App power usage

FIGURE 23-2: The battery screen.

The number and variety of items listed on the Battery screen depend on what you've been doing between charges and how many apps you're using.

Tap the BATTERY USAGE button (refer to Figure 23-2) to glean more details about which apps and device processes are consuming battery juice. You also see a nifty usage chart.

Extending battery life

A surefire way to make a battery last a good long time is to never turn on the device in the first place. But rather than let you use your Galaxy Tab as an expensive hors d'oeuvre tray, I offer a smattering of suggestions you can follow to help prolong its battery life.

Use the power saving tools: These tools are illustrated in Figure 23-2. The first tool of choice is to switch Power Saving mode from Off to Mid. If that doesn't work, choose Mac. To instantly save power, tap the SAVE POWER button, which shuts down various apps and background processes.

Dim the screen: The touchscreen display sucks down quite a lot of battery power. Though a dim screen can be more difficult to see, especially outdoors, it definitely saves battery life.

Adjust the screen timeout: Make the screen sleep at a shorter interval to save valuable battery life. Or, manually lock the tablet, especially if you're just listening to music. See Chapter 20 for information on display settings.

Turn off Bluetooth: When you're not using Bluetooth, turn it off. See Chapter 17 for information on Bluetooth, though you can turn it off easily from the Quick Actions at the top of the notifications shade.

Help and Troubleshooting

Wouldn't it be great if you could have an avuncular, Mr. Wizard type available at a moment's notice? He could just walk in and, with a happy smile on his face and a reassuring hand on your shoulder, diagnose the problem and tell you how to fix it. Never mind that such a thing would be creepy — getting helpful advice is worth it.

Fixing random and annoying problems

The next few sections present some typical problems you may encounter on your Galaxy Tab and my suggestions for a solution.

General trouble

For just about any problem or minor quirk, consider restarting the tablet: Long-press the Power Lock button and choose the Restart command from the Device Options menu. Tap the OK button. This procedure will most likely fix a majority of the annoying problems you encounter. Also see Chapter 24 for details on using the Auto Restart feature.

Signal weirdness

As you move about, the cellular signal can change. In fact, you may observe the status icon change from 4G LTE to 3G to even the dreaded 1X or — worse — nothing, depending on the strength and availability of the cellular data service.

My advice for random signal weirdness is to wait. Oftentimes, the signal comes back after a few minutes. If it doesn't, the cellular data network might be down, or you may just be in an area with lousy service. Consider changing your location.

For Wi-Fi connections, you must ensure that the Wi-Fi is set up properly and working. This process usually involves pestering the person who configured the Wi-Fi router or, in a coffee shop, bothering the cheerful person with the bad haircut who serves you coffee.

Perhaps the issue isn't with the tablet at all but rather with the Wi-Fi network. Some networks have a "lease time" after which your tablet might be disconnected. If so, follow the directions in Chapter 17 for turning off the tablet's Wi-Fi and then turn it on again. That often solves the issue.

Another problem I've heard about is that the Wi-Fi router doesn't recognize the Tab. In this case, it could be an older router that needs to be replaced. Especially if you have a Wi-Fi router over five years old, consider getting a newer model.

Music is playing and you want it to stop

It's awesome that the tablet continues to play music while you do other things. Getting the music to stop quickly, however, requires some skill. Primarily, you need skill at pulling down the notifications shade and tapping the Pause icon that appears in the currently playing song's notification.

An app has run amok

Sometimes, apps that misbehave let you know. You see a warning on the screen announcing the app's stubborn disposition. When that happens, touch the Force Quit button to shut down the app. Then say, "Whew!"

To manually shut down an app, refer to Chapter 19.

You've reached your wit's end

When all else fails, you can do the drastic thing and perform a factory data reset on your Galaxy Tab. Before committing to this step, I recommend you contact support, as described in the next section.

Refer to Chapter 21 for details on the factory data reset.

Getting support

You can use two sources of support for your Galaxy tablet. For the LTE Tab, the first source of support is your cellular provider. The second source, or the only source if you have a Wi-Fi tablet, is Samsung. Or, if you were suckered into a long-term service agreement at a Big Box store, perhaps you can try getting support from it.

Before you contact someone about support, you need to know the device's ID: Open the Settings app and choose the About Tablet category. On the right side of the screen, you see listed the Tab's model number and serial number.

For app issues, contact the developer: Bring up the app's description screen in the Play Store app. Scroll to the bottom of the screen and choose Send Email.

For issues with the Play Store, contact Google at support.google.com/googleplay.

If you have an LTE tablet and are an active mobile data subscriber, you can get help from the cellular provider. Table 23-1 lists contact information on US cellular providers.

TABLE 23-1

US Cellular Providers

Provider	Toll free	Website
AT&T	800-331-0500	www.att.com/esupport
Sprint Nextel	800-211-4727	sprint.com
T-Mobile	800-866-2453	www.t-mobile.com/Contact.aspx
Verizon	800-923-0204	verizonwireless.com/support

For hardware and other issues, you have to contact Samsung. The support website is www.samsung.com/us/support.

TIP

The fastest way to get Samsung support is to open the Settings app and choose the Help item from the left side of the screen. After you do so, a web browser tab opens, landing on the Samsung Galaxy Tab S4 online manual website. Of course, this book is far more enjoyable than that silly help website.

Valuable Galaxy Tablet Q&A

I love Q&A! Not only is it an effective way to express certain problems and solutions, but some of the questions might also cover topics I've been wanting to ask about.

"I can't turn the tablet on (or off)!"

Yes, sometimes a Galaxy Tab locks up. I even asked Samsung about this issue specifically, and the folks there told me it's impossible for a Galaxy Tab to seize! Despite their denial, I've discovered that if you press and hold down the Power Lock button for about 8 seconds, the tablet turns off or on, depending on which state it's in.

I've had a program lock the Galaxy Tab tight; even the 8-second Power Lock button trick didn't work. In that case, I waited 12 minutes or so, just letting the tablet sit there and do nothing. Then I pressed and held down the Power Lock button for about 8 seconds, and the tablet turned itself back on.

"The touchscreen doesn't work!"

The touchscreen requires a human finger for proper interaction. The tablet interprets the static potential between the human finger and the device to determine where the touchscreen is being touched.

You cannot use the touchscreen when you're wearing gloves, unless they're specially designed, static carrying gloves that claim to work on touchscreens.

The touchscreen might also fail when the battery power is low or when the tablet has been physically damaged.

TECHNICAL STUFF

I've been informed that there is an Android app for cats. This implies that the touchscreen can also interpret a feline paw for proper interaction. Either that or the cat holds a human finger in its mouth and manipulates the app that way. Because I don't have the app, I can't tell for certain.

"The battery doesn't charge!"

When the battery isn't charging, start at the source: Is it providing power? Is the cord plugged in? The cable may be damaged, so try another cable.

When charging from a USB port on a computer, ensure that the computer is turned on. Most computers don't provide USB power when they're turned off. Also, some USB ports may not supply enough power to charge the Tab. If possible, use a port on the computer console (the box) instead of a USB hub.

"The tablet gets so hot that it turns itself off!"

Yikes! An overheating gadget can be a nasty problem. Judge how hot the tablet is by seeing whether you can hold it in your hand: When it's too hot to hold, it's too hot. Or if you're using your Tab to cook an egg, it's too hot.

Turn off the tablet and let the battery cool.

If the overheating problem continues, have the tablet looked at for potential repair. The battery might need to be replaced. As far as I can tell, there's no way for you to remove and replace the battery in a Galaxy Tab.

WARNING

Do not continue to use any gizmo that's too hot! The heat damages the electronics. It can also start a fire.

"It doesn't do Landscape mode!"

Not every app takes advantage of the tablet's capability to reorient itself horizontally and vertically. For example, many games set their orientations one way and refuse to change, no matter how you hold the tablet. So, if an app doesn't go into Landscape mode, that doesn't mean anything is broken.

Confirm that the orientation lock isn't on: Check the Quick Settings on the notifications shade to ensure that the Screen Rotation item is on; otherwise, the screen doesn't reorient itself.

5

The Part of Tens

Chapter **24**

Ten Tips, Tricks, and Shortcuts

A *tip* is a small suggestion, a word of advice often spoken from experience or knowledge. A *trick*, which is something not many know, usually causes amazement or surprise. A *shortcut* is a quick way to get home, even though it crosses the old graveyard and you never quite know whether Old Man Witherspoon is the groundskeeper or a zombie.

I'd like to think that just about everything in this book is a tip, trick, or shortcut for using a Galaxy Tab. Even so, I've distilled a list of items in this chapter that are definitely worthy of note.

Make Some Multi Window Magic

Your Galaxy Tab features a multitasking tool called Multi Window. It allows you to view two apps side-by-side on the touchscreen. This view is opposed to how apps normally run, which is full-screen.

 You activate Multi Window from the Overview: To start, tap the Recent navigation icon, illustrated in the margin. Look in the Overview for open apps that feature the Multi Window icon, as illustrated in Figure 24-1. Tap that icon to open the first app, which plops into the leftmost window. The Overview remains in the right window, from which you can choose the second app.

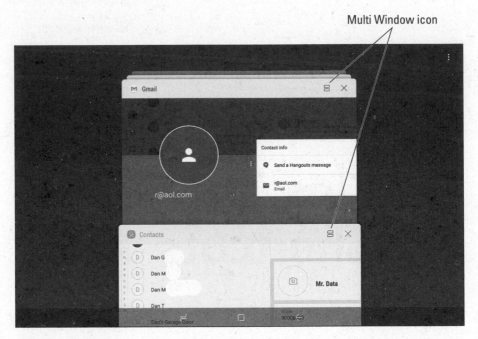

FIGURE 24-1: Finding Multi Window apps in the Overview.

Figure 24-2 illustrates two apps running side-by-side with Multi Window active. To use either app, tap in its window. You can scroll each app independently. Long-press the separator between the apps to adjust its position. Tap the center of the separator to see the pop-up, illustrated in Figure 24-2.

To exit Multi Window, long-press the separator and tap the Close (X) icon, as illustrated in Figure 24-2.

>> Only certain apps can run in Multi Window.

>> Android tablets always run multiple apps at a time. The only benefit to Multi Window is that you can view two apps at the same time.

Separator

Add app pair to the Home screen.   Swap windows.

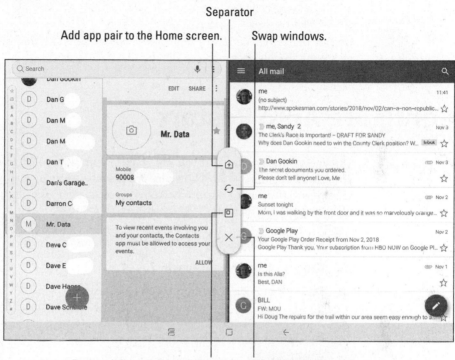

FIGURE 24-2:
Multi Window
in action.

Pop out left app into a window.   Exit Multi Window.

Snooze with Do Not Disturb Mode

I enjoy falling asleep with my Galaxy Tab handy, reading a book or playing a game. When I set it aside, however, I don't want it to bother me with notification sounds or alerts. Because I can't control when those items fly in, I activate Do Not Disturb mode. Follow these steps:

1. **Open the Settings app.**

2. **Choose Sounds and Vibration.**

3. **On the right side of the screen, choose Do Not Disturb.**

   You could just slide the master control to the On position, but I recommend instead that you schedule Do Not Disturb mode.

4. **Choose Turn On As Scheduled.**

5. **Slide the master control to the On position.**

6. **Tap the Set Schedule button to set the hours that you don't want to be bothered.**

   I prefer 10:00 PM to 6:00 AM (next day).

REMEMBER

Do Not Disturb mode mutes any alarms you've set. So if you *really* need to be up by 4 a.m., disable this mode so that you hear the alarm.

Configure Auto Restart

You know how they say that you can restart technology to fix some issues? Apparently Samsung agrees, which is why it offers the Auto Restart feature. When this feature is active, your Tab automatically restarts itself according to a given schedule. Heed these directions:

1. **Open the Settings app.**

2. **Choose General Management.**

3. **On the right side of the screen, choose Reset.**

4. **Choose Auto Restart.**

5. **Slide the master control to the On position.**

6. **Tap the Time and Day items to set when the Tab restarts.**

This setting may not cure all ills, but it may also avoid some issues when you leave your tablet on for extended periods. Because all the information on the Tab is backed up, you won't lose anything when the device restarts itself once a week.

Activate the Blue Light Filter

The light coming from the Tab's screen can be garish. In fact, the blue part of the screen's spectrum could keep you up at night or otherwise disrupt your sleep cycle. To help avoid this condition, you can activate the screen's Blue Light Filter. Obey these directions:

1. **Open the Settings app.**

2. **Choose Display.**

3. **Choose Blue Light Filter.**

   You can slide the master control to the On position to activate the filter immediately. Otherwise, tapping the Blue Light Filter item lets you set a schedule, which I prefer.

4. **Choose Turn On as Scheduled.**

5. **If prompted, tap ALLOW to access the device's location.**

   The location data helps the Tab recognize the time so that the filter can be activated automatically between sundown and sunrise.

6. **Choose Sunset to Sunrise.**

After the Blue Light Filter is active, you see the tab's color temperature fade from blue to a golden hue as the sun goes down. This change helps you better adapt to sleep when you use your Tab during the evening hours.

 You can instantly activate the Blue Light Filter by choosing the Blue Light Filter item from the Quick Actions shade.

Avoid Display Timeouts with Smart Stay

Please don't be frightened, but your Galaxy Tab knows when you're looking at it. I don't believe that it actually stares back at you, but it can look for your eyeballs. The advantage is that the display won't automatically lock as long as you're looking at the Tab, providing you've activated the Smart Stay feature.

Laying aside your fears, activate Smart Stay by following these steps:

1. **Open the Settings app.**

2. **Choose Advanced Features.**

3. **Slide the master control by Smart Stay to the On position.**

For the Smart Stay feature to work, you must look at the screen, and the area must be light enough for the Tab to see your face. (No other app should be using the front-facing camera.) I've had mixed results with this feature, though keep in mind that you can always tap the screen to prevent the display timeout from kicking in.

Watch the Tablet Dream

Does a Galaxy Tab fall asleep when the screen locks? A locked tablet seems rather restrictive, so I prefer to think of the tablet as taking a snooze. But does it dream? Of course it does! You can even see the dreams, if you've activated the Screen Saver feature — and if you keep the tablet connected to a power source or in a docking station. Heed these steps:

1. **Open the Settings app.**

2. **Choose Display.**

3. **On the right side of the screen, slide the master control by Screen Saver to the On position.**

   The Daydream feature is activated. Now you choose a daydream type.

4. **Tap the Screen Saver item to view the various types of daydreams available.**

   I'm fond of Colors.

 Some screen saver items feature the Settings icon, which can be used to customize the daydream.

The daydreaming begins when the screen would normally time-out and lock. So, if you set the tablet to lock after 5 minutes of inactivity, it daydreams instead.

>> To disrupt the tablet's dreaming, swipe the screen.

>> The tablet doesn't lock when it daydreams. To lock the tablet, press the Power Lock button.

Add Spice to Dictation

I feel that too few people use dictation, despite how handy it can be. Whether or not you use it, you might notice that it occasionally censors some of the words you utter. Perhaps you're the kind of person who won't put up with that kind of s***.

Relax, b******. You can lift the vocal censorship ban by following these steps:

1. **Open the Settings app.**

2. **Choose General.**

3. **On the right side of the screen, tap Language and Input.**

4. **Choose Onscreen Keyboard.**

5. **Choose Google Voice Typing.**

6. **Slide the master control by the option Block Offensive Words to the Off position.**

And just what are offensive words? I would think that *censorship* would be an offensive word. But no, apparently the words s***, c***, and even innocent little old a****** are deemed offensive by Google Voice. What the h***?

Restore the Apps Icon

The new, Android way to summon the Apps screen is to swipe up the Home screen, from bottom to top. Back in the cave-droid days, Android gizmos such as the Galaxy Tab featured the Apps icon; tap the Apps icon to view the Apps screen. If you want this icon back, follow these steps:

1. **Long-press a blank part of the Home screen.**

2. **Tap the Home Screen Settings icon.**

3. **Choose the Apps Button item.**

4. **Choose the option Show Apps Button.**

5. **Tap the APPLY button.**

   Tap the Home navigation icon to return to the Home screen to see what you've wrought.

 The Apps icon appears on the far right end of the Home screen dock, looking similar to what's shown in the margin.

Hide the Navigation Bar

The *navigation bar* is the strip of icons that appears at the bottom of every screen and app on the Tab, illustrated in Figure 24-3. I didn't even know the bar had a name, but that one dot on the far left bothered me.

As it turns out, that dot is used to hide the navigation bar, making it disappear just as it does in some games: Double-tap the dot, and the navigation bar, along with the navigation icons (Recent, Home, Back), disappears! Actually, the bar slides down and out of the way.

Double-tap to hide the navigation bar.

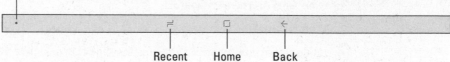

FIGURE 24-3:
The navigation
bar.

Recent   Home   Back

To see the navigation bar again, swipe up the screen slightly from the bottom. Double-tap the dot again to lock the navigation bar back into place.

**TECHNICAL
STUFF**

The button to show or hide the navigation bar can be disabled. In the Settings app: Choose Display and tap Navigation Bar on the right side of the screen. Use the master control by the Show and Hide Button item to control whether the button is visible.

Check Your Data Usage

Whether you have an LTE Tab or a Wi-Fi Tab, you can use the Data Usage screen to check Internet activity and even control how much data is sent and received.

To visit the Data Usage screen, heed these steps:

1. **Open the Settings app.**
2. **Choose Connections.**
3. **On the right side of the screen, choose Data Usage.**
4. **Choose Wi-Fi Data Usage.**

You see a graph charting data usage over time. The apps that use Wi-Fi are listed, along with their online data consumption.

The LTE Tab features a category for mobile data usage. You can adjust the red and orange limit bars to set warnings when your mobile data usage gets too close to the monthly limit.

Chapter **25**

Ten Things to Remember

Have you ever tried to tie string around your finger to remember something? I've not attempted that technique just yet. The main reason is that I keep forgetting to buy string and have no way to remind myself.

For your Galaxy Tab, some things are definitely worth remembering. From that long, long list, I've come up with ten good ones.

Summon a Recently Opened App

An Android app doesn't quit. It stays running until it's bored and shuts itself down or you turn off the Tab or you force it to quit. In the meantime, you can easily switch between running apps by tapping the Recent navigation icon. Choose an app from the Overview: Presto! It's on the screen.

TIP

If you need help remembering how the Recent button works, think of it as the same thing as the Alt+Tab key combination in Windows.

Make Quick Settings

Shortcuts exist for many of the common things you do on the Galaxy Tab. Especially for those items that can be turned on or off, you'll probably find a Quick Setting.

To view the Quick Settings, pull down the notifications shade; swipe the touchscreen from the top down. Swipe down a second time to view all the Quick Settings icons.

Use Dictation

Dictation is such a handy feature, yet I constantly forget to use it. Rather than type short messages or search text, use dictation. You can access dictation from any onscreen keyboard by touching the Dictation (microphone) icon. Speak the text; the text appears. Simple.

See Chapter 4 for dictation information.

Lock the Orientation

It's nice to be able to rotate the tablet, alternating between portrait and landscape orientations. Some apps look good one way; others, the other way. The rotation lock feature prevents the apps from switching when you don't want them to: The screen stays fixed in whichever orientation it was in when you set the orientation lock.

To set the rotation lock, pull down the notifications shade. In the Quick Settings area, locate the Auto Rotate item, similar to what's shown in the margin. Tap it to lock the orientation in a specific aspect — Landscape or Portrait. Tap the item again to unlock.

Use Keyboard Suggestions

Don't forget to take advantage of the suggestions that appear above the onscreen keyboard while you're typing text. In fact, you may not even need to type much text at all: Just keep tapping a word in the list that's presented. It's fast.

To ensure that suggestions are enabled, follow these steps:

1. **Open the Settings app.**

2. **Choose General Management.**

3. **On the right side of the screen, choose Language and Input.**

4. **Choose Onscreen Keyboard.**

5. **Choose Samsung Keyboard.**

6. **Choose Smart Typing.**

7. **Ensure that the master control by the Predictive Text option is in the On position.**

Also refer to Chapter 4 for additional information on using keyboard suggestions.

Avoid Things That Consume Lots of Battery Juice

Three items on the Galaxy Tab suck down battery power faster than a massive alien fleet is defeated by a plucky antihero who just wants the girl:

>> A bright display

>> Bluetooth

>> Navigation

Also see Chapter 23 for details on using the Tab's Battery Saver feature.

Make Phone Calls

Yeah, I know: It's not a phone. I wish it were (and Samsung might as well), but the Galaxy Tab lacks a native capability to use the cellular system for making phone calls. Even so, with apps such as Hangouts and Skype, you can make phone calls and even video-chat with others. Refer to Chapter 8 for details.

Keep Up with Your Schedule

The Calendar app can certainly be handy, reminding you of upcoming dates and generally keeping you on schedule. A great way to augment the calendar is to employ the Calendar widget on the Home screen.

The Calendar widget lists the current date and then a long list of upcoming appointments. It's a great way to check your schedule, especially when you use your tablet all the time. I recommend sticking the Calendar widget right on the main Home screen.

See Chapter 19 for information on adding widgets to the Home screen; Chapter 15 covers using the Calendar app.

Snap a Pic of That Contact

Here's something I forget: Whenever you're with one of your contacts, take the person's picture. Sure, some people are bashful, but most folks are flattered. The idea is to build up your Contacts list so that every contact has a photo.

REMEMBER

When taking a picture, be sure to show it to the person before you assign it to the contact. Let her decide whether it's good enough. Or, if you just want to be rude, assign a crummy-looking picture. Heck, you don't even have to do that: Just take a random picture of anything and assign it to a contact. A plant. A rock. Your cat. Just keep in mind that the tablet can take a contact's picture the next time you meet up with that person.

See Chapter 12 for more information on using the tablet's camera. Assigning contact pictures is covered in Chapter 6.

Enter Location Information for Your Events

When you create an event for the Calendar app, remember to enter the event location. You can type either an address (if you know it) or the name of the location. The key is to type the text as you would type it in the Maps app when searching for a location. That way, you can touch the event location and the tablet displays it on the touchscreen. Finding an appointment couldn't be easier.

>> See Chapter 11 for more information about the Maps app.

>> See Chapter 15 for details about the Calendar app.

Index

About the Author

Dan Gookin has been writing about technology for nearly three decades. He combines his love of writing with his gizmo fascination to create books that are informative, entertaining, and not boring. Having written over 160 titles with 12 million copies in print translated into over 30 languages, Dan can attest that his method of crafting computer tomes seems to work.

Perhaps his most famous title is the original *DOS For Dummies*, published in 1991. It became the world's fastest-selling computer book, at one time moving more copies per week than the *New York Times* number-one bestseller (though, as a reference, it could not be listed on the Times' Best Sellers list). That book spawned the entire line of *For Dummies* books, which remains a publishing phenomenon to this day.

Dan's most popular titles include *PCs For Dummies*, *Laptops For Dummies*, and *Microsoft Word For Dummies*. He also maintains the vast and helpful website www.wambooli.com.

Dan holds a degree in Communications/Visual Arts from the University of California, San Diego. He lives in the Pacific Northwest, where he enjoys spending time annoying people who deserve it.

Publisher's Acknowledgments

Acquisitions Editor: Katie Mohr

Senior Project Editor: Paul Levesque

Copy Editor: Becky Whitney

Editorial Assistant: Matthew Lowe

Sr. Editorial Assistant: Cherie Case

Production Editor: Siddique Shaik

Cover Image: Courtesy of Dan Gookin; background © Iscatel/Shutterstock

Take dummies with you everywhere you go!

Whether you are excited about e-books, want more from the web, must have your mobile apps, or are swept up in social media, dummies makes everything easier.

Find us online!

dummies.com

dummies®
A Wiley Brand

Leverage the power

Dummies is the global leader in the reference category and one of the most trusted and highly regarded brands in the world. No longer just focused on books, customers now have access to the dummies content they need in the format they want. Together we'll craft a solution that engages your customers, stands out from the competition, and helps you meet your goals.

Advertising & Sponsorships

Connect with an engaged audience on a powerful multimedia site, and position your message alongside expert how-to content. Dummies.com is a one-stop shop for free, online information and know-how curated by a team of experts.

- Targeted ads
- Video
- Email Marketing

- Microsites
- Sweepstakes sponsorship

20 MILLION PAGE VIEWS EVERY SINGLE MONTH

15 MILLION UNIQUE VISITORS PER MONTH

43% OF ALL VISITORS ACCESS THE SITE VIA THEIR MOBILE DEVICES

700,000 NEWSLETTER SUBSCRIPTIONS TO THE INBOXES OF *300,000* UNIQUE INDIVIDUALS EVERY WEEK

# of dummies

Custom Publishing

Reach a global audience in any language by creating a solution that will differentiate you from competitors, amplify your message, and encourage customers to make a buying decision.

- Apps
- Books
- eBooks
- Video
- Audio
- Webinars

Brand Licensing & Content

Leverage the strength of the world's most popular reference brand to reach new audiences and channels of distribution.

For more information, visit dummies.com/biz

PERSONAL ENRICHMENT

Staying Sharp	Facebook	Guitar	Investing	Beekeeping	Digital Photography
9781119187790	9781119179030	9781119293354	9781119293347	9781119310068	9781119235606
USA $26.00	USA $21.99	USA $24.99	USA $22.99	USA $22.99	USA $24.99
CAN $31.99	CAN $25.99	CAN $29.99	CAN $27.99	CAN $27.99	CAN $29.99
UK £19.99	UK £16.99	UK £17.99	UK £16.99	UK £16.99	UK £17.99

Meditation	Pregnancy	Samsung Galaxy S7	iPhone	Crocheting	Nutrition
9781119251163	9781119235491	9781119279952	9781119283133	9781119287117	9781119130246
USA $24.99	USA $26.99	USA $24.99	USA $24.99	USA $24.99	USA $22.99
CAN $29.99	CAN $31.99	CAN $29.99	CAN $29.99	CAN $29.99	CAN $27.99
UK £17.99	UK £19.99	UK £17.99	UK £17.99	UK £16.99	UK £16.99

PROFESSIONAL DEVELOPMENT

Windows 10	AutoCAD	Excel 2016	QuickBooks 2017	macOS Sierra	LinkedIn	Windows 10 All-in-One
9781119311041	9781119255796	9781119293439	9781119281467	9781119280651	9781119251132	9781119310563
USA $24.99	USA $39.99	USA $26.99	USA $26.99	USA $29.99	USA $24.99	USA $34.00
CAN $29.99	CAN $47.99	CAN $31.99	CAN $31.99	CAN $35.99	CAN $29.99	CAN $41.99
UK £17.99	UK £27.99	UK £19.99	UK £19.99	UK £21.99	UK £17.99	UK £24.99

SharePoint 2016	Fundamental Analysis	Networking	Office 2016	Office 365	Salesforce.com	Coding
9781119181705	9781119263593	9781119257769	9781119293477	9781119265313	9781119239314	9781119293323
USA $29.99	USA $26.99	USA $29.99	USA $26.99	USA $24.99	USA $29.99	USA $29.99
CAN $35.99	CAN $31.99	CAN $35.99	CAN $31.99	CAN $29.99	CAN $35.99	CAN $35.99
UK £21.99	UK £19.99	UK £21.99	UK £19.99	UK £17.99	UK £21.99	UK £21.99

dummies.com

dummies
A Wiley Brand

Learning Made Easy

ACADEMIC

9781119293576
USA $19.99
CAN $23.99
UK £15.99

9781119293637
USA $19.99
CAN $23.99
UK £15.99

9781119293491
USA $19.99
CAN $23.99
UK £15.99

9781119293460
USA $19.99
CAN $23.99
UK £15.99

9781119293590
USA $19.99
CAN $23.99
UK £15.99

9781119215844
USA $26.99
CAN $31.99
UK £19.99

9781119293378
USA $22.99
CAN $27.99
UK £16.99

9781119293521
USA $19.99
CAN $23.99
UK £15.99

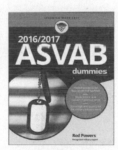

9781119239178
USA $18.99
CAN $22.99
UK £14.99

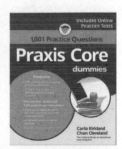

9781119263883
USA $26.99
CAN $31.99
UK £19.99

Available Everywhere Books Are Sold

dummies.com

Small books for big imaginations

GETTING STARTED WITH Coding
Get Creative with Code!
Camille McCue, PhD

9781119177173
USA $9.99
CAN $9.99
UK £8.99

MODDING Minecraft™
Build Your Own Minecraft Mods!
Sarah Guthals, PhD
Stephen Foster, PhD
Lindsey Handley, PhD

9781119177272
USA $9.99
CAN $9.99
UK £8.99

MAKING YouTube® VIDEOS
Star in Your Own Video!
Nick Willoughby

9781119177241
USA $9.99
CAN $9.99
UK £8.99

DESIGNING Digital Games
Create Games with Scratch™!
Derek Breen

9781119177210
USA $9.99
CAN $9.99
UK £8.99

GETTING STARTED WITH Raspberry Pi®
Program Your Raspberry Pi®!
Richard Wentk

9781119262657
USA $9.99
CAN $9.99
UK £6.99

EXPERIMENTING WITH Science
Think, Test, and Learn!

9781119291336
USA $9.99
CAN $9.99
UK £6.99

CREATING Digital Animations
Animate Stories with Scratch!
Derek Breen

9781119233527
USA $9.99
CAN $9.99
UK £6.99

GETTING STARTED WITH Engineering
Think Like an Engineer!
Camille McCue, PhD

9781119291220
USA $9.99
CAN $9.99
UK £6.99

WRITING Computer Code
Learn the Language of Computers!
Chris Minnick and Eva Holland

9781119177302
USA $9.99
CAN $9.99
UK £8.99

Unleash Their Creativity

dummies.com